25th Joint Workshop on Linguistics and Language Processing (JWLLP-25)

Hong Kong, China
1 – 3 December 2018

ISBN: 978-1-5108-8907-1

Printed from e-media with permission by:

Curran Associates, Inc.
57 Morehouse Lane
Red Hook, NY 12571

Some format issues inherent in the e-media version may also appear in this print version.

Printed by Curran Associates, Inc. (2019)

For permission requests, please contact the Association for Computational Linguistics at the address below.

Association for Computational Linguistics
209 N. Eighth Street
Stroudsburg, Pennsylvania 18360

Phone: 1-570-476-8006
Fax: 1-570-476-0860

acl@aclweb.org

Additional copies of this publication are available from:

Curran Associates, Inc.
57 Morehouse Lane
Red Hook, NY 12571 USA
Phone: 845-758-0400
Fax: 845-758-2633
Email: curran@proceedings.com
Web: www.proceedings.com

TABLE OF CONTENTS

Foreword

The 32nd Pacific Asia Conference on Language, Information and Computation (PACLIC) was held at The Hong Kong Polytechnic University on December 1-3, 2018, in conjunction with the 25th Joint Workshop on Linguistics and Language Processing (JWLLP) and the 5th Workshop on Asian Translation (WAT). JWLLP was held as a special session within PACLIC, and WAT was held separately at the same time as PACLIC. One of the goals of PACLIC is to emphasize and foster interdisciplinary cross-talk between linguistic and computational research. For example, while the papers presented at that conference can roughly be categorized into "linguistic" and "computational" papers, the conference organizers intentionally avoided arranging them into "linguistic" and "computational" sessions; rather, almost all the oral and poster sessions were arranged to include both types of papers, to create more opportunities for people of these backgrounds to learn about one another's work.

We received 194 submissions from around the world for PACLIC-32, JWLLP-25 and WAT-5 together. For the main conference and JWLLP workshop, 57 papers (32.2%) were accepted for oral presentations and 50 (28.2%) for poster presentations; for WAT-5 workshop, 17 papers were accepted. For these papers, we received reviews from over 180 ad-hoc reviewers outside of the programme committee (plus reviews from members of the programme committee). We would like to express our sincere gratitude to all the authors who submitted their work and to all the reviewers who volunteered their time for reviewing. Without you, this conference could not have been possible.

We were also fortunate to have keynote talks by Laurent Prévot (Aix Marseille Université), Emily M. Bender (University of Washington), and Alan C. L. Yu (University of Chicago), as well as invited talks by Helen Mei-Ling Meng (University of Hong Kong), Yashuhiro Katagiri (Future University Hakodate), Qi Su (Peking University), and Thi Minh Huyen Nguyen (VNU University of Science). Finally, we would like to thank the PACLIC Steering Committee and the local co-chairs (David C. S. Li, Qin Lu, and Hans J. Ladegaard) for their support.

Chu-ren Huang & Min Zhang (Programme Committee Honorary Chairs)
Yu-Yin Hsu & Guohong Fu (Programme Committee Chairs)
The PACLIC 32 Programme Committee

Reviewers for PACLIC and JWLLP

Kathleen Ahrens
Alice Mae M. Arbon
Wirote Aroonmanakun
Laurent Besacier
Philippe Blache
Allan Bravo Borra
Marut Buranarach
Damir Cavar
Yung-Hsiang Shawn Chang
Alvin Cheng-Hsien Chen
Chun-Yin Doris Chen
Kuang-Hua Chen
Lyu Chen
Qian Chen
Qincai Chen
Si Chen
Chengyao Chen
Charibeth Cheng
Emmanuele Chersoni
Candice Cheung
Sung-Kwon Choi
Eunjin Chun
Jin-Woo Chung
Siaw-Fong Chung
Katrina Connell
Volker Dellwo
Hongwei Ding
Xiao Ding
Youngah Do
Li Dong
Sicong Dong
Jianyong Duan
Jianyong Duan
Astrid Ensslin
Alex Fang
Guohong Fu
Helena Gao
Thomas Grano
Yanhui Gu
Yasunari Harada
Choochart Haruechaiyasak
Kiyota Hashimoto
Jeffery Holliday
Munpyo Hong
I-Ta Chris Hsieh
Miao-Ling Hsieh
Shu-Kai Hsieh
Hsu-Wen Huang
Jiangping Huang
Rui-heng Ray Huang
Joel Ilao
Suyueon Im
Peng Jin
Tomoyuki Kajiwara
Xiaohua Ke
Ji-Hye Kim
Jongbok Kim
Sunghwan Mac Kim
Natalia Klyueva
Mamoru Komachi
Fang Kong
Valia Kordoni
Pei-Jung Kuo
Oi Yee Kwong
Huei-Ling Lai
Olivia Lam
Albert Lee
Peppina Lee
Yong-Hun Lee
Sang-im Lee-Kim
Baoli Li
Dong Li
Fei Li
Junhui Li
Ru Li
Wenjie Li
Zhenghua Li
Shuilong Liang
Wei-wen Roger Liao
Dongsik Lim
Jingxia Lin
Yuhan Lin
Bingquan Liu
Chao-Lin Liu
Jiangming Liu
Jyi-Shane Liu
Kang Liu
Meichun Liu
Te-Hsin Liu
Yijia Liu
Yunfei Long
Lu Lu
Qin Lu
Wei Lu
Yu-an Lu
Minh-Thang Luong
Chen Lyu
Yajuan Lyu
Xingcheng Ma
Erlyn Manguilimotan
Yuji Matsumoto
Fandong Meng
Yoshiki Mori
James Myers
Natchanan Natpratan
Ponrudee Netisopakul
Jian-Yun Nie
Nathaniel Oco
Ethel Ong
Chutamanee Onsuwan
Yohei Oseki
Ryo Otoguro
Jong C. Park
Stephen Politzer-Ahles
Nattama Pongpairoj
Haoliang Qi
Tao Qian
Zhen Qin
Xipeng Qiu
Yafeng Ren
Jr. Callanta Raga Rodolfo
Luke Rudge
Pavel Rychl
Byong-Rae Ryu
Jing Shao
Liang Shuailong
Shu-Ing Shyu
Melanie Siegel
Pornsiri Singhapreecha
Wei Song
Virach Sornlertlamvanich
Keh-Yih Su
Chengjie Sun
Leif Romeritch Syliongka
Tianyong Tak-Sum Wong
Zhi Tang
Hongyin Tao
Qian Tao
Zhiyang Teng
Satoshi Tomioka
Ming-Feng Tsai
Yuen-Hsien Tseng
Aline Villavicencio
Itamar Kastner Wang
YuChun Wang
Zhongqing Wang
Zhongyu Wei

Tak-Sum Wong
Dekai Wu
Chen-hui Wu
Doreen Wu
Jiun-Shiung Wu
Ming Xiang
Shufeng Xiong
Hongzhi Xu
Ruifeng Xu
Nianwen Xue
Yun Xue
Cheng-Zen Yang
Chung-Lin Martin Yang
Jie Yang
Liner Yang
Muyun Yang
Foongha Yap
Satoru Yokoyama
James Hye Suk Yoon
Alan Yu
Liang-Chih Yu
Xue Yun
Hongying Zan
Caicai Zhang
Chengzhi Zhang
Jiajun Zhang
Meishan Zhang
Niina Ning Zhang
Peng Zhang
Hai Zhao
Deyu Zhou
Hao Zhou
Junsheng Zhou
Muhua Zhu
Michael Zock

How do non-tastes taste?

A corpus-based study on Chinese people's perception of spicy and numbing food

Sicong Dong
The Hong Kong Polytechnic University - Peking University Research Centre on Chinese Linguistics
szechungtung@gmail.com

Yin Zhong
Department of Chinese and Bilingual Studies
The Hong Kong Polytechnic University
beth.zhong@connect.polyu.hk

Chu-Ren Huang
Department of Chinese and Bilingual Studies
The Hong Kong Polytechnic University
churen.huang@polyu.edu.hk

Abstract

'Spicy' 辣 and 'Numbing' 麻 have long been known as tastes by Chinese people, though they are proved to be chemesthesis by neuroscientists. To examine the conceptualised perception of 'spicy' and 'numbing' among Chinese people, a corpus was compiled in the *Sketch Engine* which consists of comments on spicy and numbing food in *Dazhong Dianping*, the most popular food review website in China. After analysing 'spicy' and 'numbing' words and their collocations, we found evidence that they are indeed perceived as chemesthesis by Chinese people. First, these two senses are closely related to hurt and irritation which are among the properties of chemesthesis. Secondly, verbs that are semantically related to hurt and irritation collocate with 'spicy' and 'numbing', but not with the basic five taste properties. Thirdly, some collocations are found in accordance with the mechanisms of capsaicin in various aspects. In addition, semantic extension of the morphemes meaning 'spicy' and 'numbing' in Sinitic languages are mainly based on the meaning of irritation. Apart from that, according to the data, 'spicy' and 'numbing' interact with taste and smell sensations to some extent but have a loose relation with 'mouthfeel'. A synaesthetic account of transfer from taste to touch is provided for the divergence of 'spicy' and 'numbing' being deemed tastes while perceived as chemesthesis.

1 Introduction

The concept of 五味 *wuwei* 'five tastes' has been a long-held view on gustatory (taste) sense by Chinese people. As in the classic text *Lüshi Chunqiu* cited below, those five tastes are *sweet*, *sour*, *bitter*, *spicy* and *salty*. Due to the close relation of food and medicine in Chinese culture, 五味 *wuwei* also plays an important role in traditional Chinese medicine that those five tastes are believed to have different healing functions and are related to different internal organs.

五味三材... 调和之事，必以甘酸苦辛咸...
Among the five tastes and three materials... In the matter of blending [tastes], the sweet, the sour, the bitter, the spicy and the salty must be used. (吕氏春秋 *Lüshi Chunqiu*, 3rd century B.C.)

Therefore, 辛 *xin* or 辣 *la* (used more frequently in Modern Chinese), 'spicy', is one of the traditionally accepted tastes in China, as exemplified by a lexicalised term 酸甜苦辣 *suan-tian-ku-la* 'sour-sweet-bitter-spicy' in Modern Chinese, meaning all kinds of tastes, and also joys and sorrows of life metaphorically. Based on

32nd Pacific Asia Conference on Language, Information and Computation
The 25th Joint Workshop on Linguistics and Language Processing
Hong Kong, 1-3 December 2018

ShuoWenJieZi Zhu (Duan, 1815), 辛 *xin* has its most likely original meaning of serious punishment of cutting parts out of human body in ancient China. The severe pain caused by which was very likely to relate to the taste sense of 辛 *xin*, although most Chinese people might not realise this original meaning in later uses of 辛 *xin* and 辣 *la*.

Besides spicy food, Chinese people have a very long history of eating Sichuan (or Szechuan) Pepper (花椒 *huajiao*), which creates a numbing feeling (麻 *ma*), and is also considered as a taste sense by Chinese people. This can be supported by the following expressions when doing exact search in Google, where 麻 *ma* is frequently coordinated with *sour*, *sweet*, *bitter* and *spicy* (accessed 22 June 2018, with result numbers indicated in the brackets): '酸甜苦麻辣' (11300), '酸甜苦辣麻' (7730), '甜酸苦辣麻' (4170), '甜酸苦麻辣' (202). As a matter of fact, Sichuan pepper, the use of which can be traced in *Shijing* (11th - 7th century B.C.), was one of the main spices that ancient Chinese used to produce the 辛 *xin* 'spicy' flavour, while the use of chilli pepper came much later, with the first written record in the mid- and late Ming dynasty (1368 – 1644) (Zhao, 2006, p.346-350). Thus, 辛 *xin* might probably also denote the numbing feeling in Classical Chinese.

Chilli pepper is now widely used in China, but the regions that also consume Sichuan pepper, i.e. with a 麻辣 *mala* 'numbing-and-spicy' cuisine, are mainly in Sichuan Province and Chongqing City, which used to be part of Sichuan until 1997. Due to the heavy usage of chilli pepper and Sichuan pepper, the spicy and numbing flavours are more prominent in Sichuan cuisine than other regions in China (Zhao, 2003, p.46). According to Dunlop (2008), the strange, fizzing effect of Sichuan pepper, paired with the heat of chillies, is one of the hallmarks of modern Sichuanese cookery.

Although Chinese people treat spicy and numbing as tastes, modern science shows that they not belong to the gustatory sense, a sensory modality in which the basic taste qualities could be found in the taste buds on the tongue. Instead, they belong to 'common chemical sense', a kind of sense as distinct and well defined as smell or taste (Parker, 1912), or currently more often referred to as 'chemesthesis', a coined term indicating the chemical sensitivity of the skin and mucous membranes derives primarily from nerve fibres that belong to the sensory systems classically defined as touch, temperature, and pain (Green, 1996; 2016). In particular, capsaicin, the primary pungent compound in chilli pepper, is related to the pain and warming sensations; and sanshool, the primary pungent compound in Sichuan pepper, is responsible for the induced tactile and thermal sensitivity (Bryant & Mezine, 1999). Hagura *et al.* (2013) also found that the frequency-specific tactile channel is shared between Sichuan pepper and mechanical vibration, at around 50 Hz.

The spicy and numbing feelings caused by chilli pepper and Sichuan pepper, traditionally known as taste sense in China, shall belong to 'chemesthesis', which, together with taste, smell and mouthfeel, contributes to the integrated sensory impressions evoked in the oral cavity called *flavour* (Mouritsen & Styrbæk, 2014, p.5). Therefore, it will be interesting to address the following questions in this study:

a. How do Chinese people perceive 'spicy' and 'numbing' in the food? and,
b. Do Chinese people perceive them as 'taste sense' like what we call them, or as 'chemesthesis' as what they really are?

2 Methodology

First, 5 hot pot (火锅 *huoguo*) and 5 skewer hot pot (串串香 *chuanchuanxiang*) restaurants in Chongqing and Chengdu each, i.e. 20 in total, are chosen in the website *Dazhong Dianping* (大众点评)[1] according to the rates of positive comments. This is because Chongqing and Chengdu are the two biggest cities in the core region of Sichuan cuisine which are unique for their spicy and numbing flavour, and the two kinds of chosen food contain the most concentrated spicy and numbing flavour since other Sichuan cuisine restaurants would serve various dishes that are not spicy or numbing. Only the positive comments are chosen because the negative comments of the popular restaurants are much fewer than the positive ones. The categories selected in *Dazhong Dianping* for Chongqing restaurants include 'Chongqing hot pot' and 'skewer hot pot' under the category of 'hot pot'; while 'Sichuan hot pot/numbing-and-spicy hotpot' under the category of 'hot pot' and

[1] Accessed at http://www.dianping.com/

'skewer hot pot' for Chengdu are chosen. In the refining stage of the selected restaurants, two of them were replaced by the succeeding two lower-ranking ones because their food does not match the criteria of this study.

Secondly, a third-party web crawler *Octoparse* (八爪鱼 *Bazhuayu*) is used to scrape the data from the website automatically. A tagged corpus is compiled in the *Sketch Engine*[2] (Kilgarriff *et al.*, 2014) (collected on 17 June 2018). A total of 9,141 comments have been collected, consisting of 1,255,649 Chinese characters, 723,502 words and 866,968 tokens.

Thirdly, two major functions of the *Sketch Engine* were used in the study. One is 'Word Sketch', which is used to generate collocations. Results can be sorted by score or frequency. The scores of every item in the collocations will be provided throughout this paper and the scores are computed as follows:

$$14 + \log_2 \text{Dice}\left(\frac{||w_1, R, w_2||}{||w_1, R, *||}, \frac{||w_1, R, w_2||}{||*, R, w_2||}\right) = 14 + \log_2 \frac{2 \cdot ||w_1, R, w_2||}{||w_1, R, *|| + ||*, R, w_2||}$$

The other one is 'Keywords', which is used to identify individual words (tokens) which appear more frequently in the focus corpus than in the reference corpus, which is *Chinese Web 2011 (zhTenTen11, Stanford tagger)* in our study. The keyness score of a word is calculated according to the following formula:

$$\frac{fpm_{focus} + n}{fpm_{ref} + n}$$

3 Spicy and numbing are perceived as chemesthesis

Contrary to the common belief among Chinese people, the spicy and numbing flavours are perceived as chemesthesis but not tastes, as manifested by our data. This finding can be supported by the following arguments.

3.1 Collocations with 'hurt' and 'irritation'

In Table 1, the words for spicy and numbing are collocated with words meaning 'hurt' and 'irritation' which will make people feel uncomfortable or even painful, as presented in the first two rows. The words shown in the rest rows suggest that verbs meaning different kinds of hurt or irritation can go with various body parts and the spicy and numbing flavours. It indicates that Chinese people can realise spicy and numbing are associated with chemesthesis, and they can use language to describe such feelings explicitly.

辣味 spicy taste	冲 irritating 11.67, 烧心 burn heart 11.67
麻 numbing	刺激 irritation 9.41
伤 hurt	胃 stomach 11.19,嗓子 throat 10.82
烧 burn	胃 stomach 10.82,脸 face 10.14, 嘴 mouth 9.27, 肚子 belly 9.06
熏 smoke	辣油 chilli oil 12.68, 辣椒 chilli pepper 8.91
呛 irritating	嗓子 throat 12.29, 鼻子 nose 11.83
冲 irritating	鼻 nose 10.82
刺激 irritation	爽辣 refreshingly spicy 12.68, 辣度 spicy degree 9.75,麻 numbing 9.41, 辣 spicy 9.24, 麻辣 numbing and spicy 5.23

Table 1: Collocations with hurt and irritation

3.2 Collocations with verbs

Many verbs in our corpus as listed in Table 2, have meanings of reducing the degree of intense feelings such as 缓解 'to relieve' etc., the action or ability to tolerate negative experience such as 承受 'to bear' etc., the ability or courage to do something such as 敢 'dare' etc., to accommodate to unfamiliar things such as 惯 'get used to', to lead to negative results such as 导致 'to lead to', and negative actions such as 怕 'to fear', 哭 'to cry' and 死 'to die', etc. However, those verbs collocated with 'spicy' and 'numbing' in our corpus could not find association with 酸(味/度) 'sour (taste/degree)', 甜(味/度) 'sweet (taste/degree)', 苦(味/度) 'bitter (taste/degree)', 咸(味/度) 'salty (taste/degree)', 鲜(味/度) 'umami (taste/degree)' in the corpus *Chinese Web 2011 (zhTenTen11, Stanford tagger)* in the *Sketch Engine*. It further proves that spicy and numbing feelings have been perceived differently from those 'true' taste properties, and they are closely related to the irritation of chemesthesis. Thus, when spicy and numbing foods are served in certain quantities, intense feelings need to be relieved. Besides that, spicy and numbing feelings are hard to tolerate,

[2] Accessed at https://the.sketchengine.co.uk/

courage is required if people are not used to these feelings, and negative feelings like *fear*, *crying*, and *death* will be expressed.[3]

辣味 spicy taste	稍减 slightly reduce 9.19, 缓解 relieve 9.19, 解解 relieve 9.14, 接受 accept 9.1
辣 spicy	解 relieve 11.56, 怕 fear 9.71, 哭 cry 9.59, 死 die 9.22, 能吃 can eat 7.99, 解解 relieve 7.7, 死人 die human 7.66
辣度 spicy degree	缓冲 buffer 10.68, 承受 bear 10.68, 接受 accept 10.09, 减缓 slow down 9.41, 忍 endure 9.38, 挑战 challenge 9.27, 受得了 bear 8.81
麻 numbing	惯 get used to 10.51, 刺激 irritate 9.41, 不怕 not scare 9.16, 淌汗 sweat 8.93, 导致 lead to 8.82
辣椒 chilli pepper	敢 dare 8.43
花椒 Sichuan pepper	接受 accept 8.55
刺激 irritation	饱受 suffer 11.19

Table 2: Verbs closely related to 'spicy' and 'numbing'

3.3 Collocations in line with the mechanisms of capsaicin

When we glance over the comments, some findings seem quite interesting. (1) Many people think the degree or intensity of spicy and numbing is much higher at the later stage of dining. (2) Some non-local people are not used to the spicy and numbing flavours of hot pot and skewer hot pot. (3) Many diners tend to consume other sweet or cold food to relieve the intense feeling caused by spiciness. With the collocations and keyword lists, these observations are considered valid, and can all be supported by the previous research on the mechanisms of capsaicin, which bolsters the claim that spicy and numbing are perceived as chemesthesis.

The collocations in Table 3 show that the flavours of spicy and numbing are not so strong at the beginning (开始), but the more (越) you eat (吃), the heavier they get (变重), and subsequently (后面) they will slowly (慢慢) come out (出来), appear (显现) and release (释放). This is because compared to tastes, capsaicin has a slow onset and persists for prolonged periods, and successive capsaicin stimuli at short intervals will continue to produce increasing irritation in the burn intensity, which is a phenomenon known as 'sensitisation' (Prescott & Stevenson, 1995).

辣味 spicy taste	出来 come out 9.93, 后面 later 9.93, 慢慢 slowly 9.35, 显现 appear 9.12, 释放 release 9.04
辣 spicy	开始 beginning 7.92
辣度 spicy degree	显露 appear 8.81
麻味 numbing taste	变重 get heavier 12.68, 后面 later 9.27
麻 numbing	后面 later 8.01
吃 eat	越 more 11.08

Table 3: Collocations concerning the latency of onset and time course

According to the collocations shown in Table 4, non-local people are not used to the heavy spicy and numbing flavours, and have to choose the suitable spicy degree, frequently slightly spicy. This phenomenon may be due to 'desensitisation', which occurs when the interval of stimulation is relatively long and subsequent stimuli of capsaicin are perceived as less intense. Another possibility is that the greater range of sensation intensities experienced by frequent chilli users may make them judge capsaicin burn as less intense than infrequent users (Prescott & Stevenson, 1995).

外地 non-local	吃不得辣 cannot eat spicy 13.99, 辣度 spicy degree 10.91, 微辣 slightly spicy 8.91, 适合 suit 7.78
惯 get used to	(口味儿)重的 (flavour) heavy 11.67, 麻 numbing 10.51, 不 not 7.87

Table 4: Collocations concerning the discomfort of non-local people

[3] The verb 死 'to die' also appears in the collocations with taste words, but the scores are all under 1.0, much lower than its collocation with 辣 'spicy' (2.83 in *Chinese Web 2011* and 9.22 in our corpus). Besides, some of the verbs or similar verbs can also collocate with 苦 'bitter', such as 饱受 'to suffer' 9.25, 忍受 'to endure' 6.35, 缓解 'to relieve' 2.29, etc. However, in the corresponding contexts, 苦 'bitter' is used with the meaning of suffering of life but not one of the five tastes.

Lastly, as a corpus based on comments on spicy and numbing food, it seems unusual to have the following terms of sweet or cold food in the top 25 key single words and top 25 key multi-words (keyness scores attached): 冰粉 'icy jelly' 599.18, 糍粑 'glutinous rice cake' 475.95, 红糖糍粑 'brown sugar glutinous rice cake' 419.7, 银耳汤 'tremella soup' 145.01. These kinds of food are actually used to reduce the intensity of irritation. A somewhat funny thing is that people who go to eat spicy food are inclined to relieve the spiciness, as discussed in section 3.2, and what they use to achieve this is almost sweet or cold food, more examples can be found in the collocations of 解辣 'to relieve spiciness': 豆奶 'soy milk' 11.19, 凉爽 'cool' 11.09, 冰冰凉凉 'icy and cool' 10.75, 酸梅 'sour plum' 10.68, 甜 'sweet' 10.6, 汤圆 'glutinous rice ball' 9.64, 冰 'ice' 9.44, 红糖 'brown sugar' 9.32, 冰粉 'icy jelly' 9.19.[4] This phenomenon could be explained by the findings that the burning sensation produced by capsaicin can be reduced by lower temperatures and sweetness (Prescott & Stevenson, 1995; Mouritsen & Styrbæk, 2017, p.20).

3.4 Evidence from the Sinitic languages

Rakova (2003, pp.39-40) investigates 8 European languages together with English, to see what words they use to refer to the spicy flavour. She suggests that the words can mainly be divided into two groups, spicy = hot, and spicy = sharp. It means that words for the spicy flavour are also words for sensations caused by either noxious thermal or mechanical stimuli. To make a comparison, we investigate Mandarin Chinese and 42 Sinitic languages or Chinese dialects using dictionaries[5]. The basic meaning of 辣 *la* 'spicy' is the irritating flavour, and 麻 *ma* 'numbing' refers to the numb feeling in the tongue/mouth or other parts of human body, and the semantic extension of the morphemes 辣 *la* and 麻 *ma* also display relations with the properties of irritating chemesthesis.

First, meanings of 辣 *la* and 麻 *ma* are all negative or neutral, except only one positive meaning 能干'competent' in Nanchang dialect. 辣 *la* in 44.2% of the languages means 辣味刺激 'to irritate by the spicy flavour', also in 44.2% of the languages means 狠毒 'vicious', which are based on the offensive pain-causing properties of spicy. 麻 *ma* in some languages has meanings like 办事迟缓, 拖拉 'tardy' (Haikou), 微醉 'drunk' (Chengdu), 不沉着, 显得忙乱 'flustered' (Suzhou), 狂妄自大 'arrogant' (Yangzhou) and 哄骗 'to deceive' (Chengdu and Guiyang), all of which relate to the numbness in the process of moving or thinking.

Secondly, 辣 *la* is related to pain or warming in compound words or phrases, such as 火辣辣 'hot or painful' (Mandarin), 热辣辣 'hot' (Guangzhou), 辣火 'chilli pepper' (Suzhou), 辣化化 'burning and prickling' (Hangzhou), 麻辣火烧 'burning pain' (Changsha).

Thirdly, some compound words use 麻 *ma* to demonstrate the vibration property of numbing, as in 麻苏苏 'spasm feeling caused by fear' (Lanzhou). In addition, some cases using 辣 *la* can have meanings like 泼辣 'termagant' (Mandarin) or 辣手 'tricky' (Yinchuan, etc.), which are also derived from the offensive pain-causing properties of spicy as chemesthesis.

4 Interaction with other senses

When eating and enjoying food, it is the integration of the combined senses that produces what we think of as *flavour* (Mouritsen & Styrbæk, 2017, p.23). Although spicy and numbing are not tastes, they do interplay with tastes, as well as with some other senses.

4.1 Hurt and irritation to sensory organs

The first kind of interaction is not in the least peaceful: Spiciness and numbness hurt all kinds of sensory organs. In the collocations of different sensory organs, shown in Table 5, we can find that except for the burning and numbing irritation, hot pots may also make diners' mouths malfunctioning or swelling, or even cause problems in their ears and eyes.

[4] 豆奶 'soy milk', 酸梅(汤) 'sour plum (juice)' and 汤圆 'glutinous rice ball' are almost always served with sugar in Chongqing and Chengdu.

[5] The data of the 42 languages are almost based on *Xiandai Hanyu Fangyan Da Cidian* [Great Dictionary of Modern Chinese Dialects] edited by Rong Li, with one exception of *Lanzhou Fangyan Cidian* [Dictionary of Lanzhou Dialect] written by Wenxuan Zhang and Chao Mo. The detailed list is not provided here due to limited space.

嘴巴 mouth	冰块敷 ice compress 12.68, 失去 lose 11.61, (不)好使 (cannot) function well 10.82, 爆炸 explode 10.6, (吃不)消 cannot bear 10.3, 麻 numbing 9.83
嘴 mouth	肿肿 swell 10.41, 肿 swell 10.41, 烧 burn 9.27, 麻 numbing 8.71
嘴皮 lip	翻过来 turn over 13.41, 发麻 numbing 11.83
嘴唇 lip	不行 cannot stand 10
舌头 **tongue**	打结 knot 11.83, 发麻 numbing 11.09, 麻 numbing 9.02
鼻子 **nose**	呛 irritate 11.83
鼻 **nose**	冲 irritate 12.68
耳朵 **ear**	听(不见) (cannot) hear 10.09
眼睛 eye	熏 smoke 12.09, 熏到 smoke 11.41, 睁(不开) (cannot) open 11, 出汗 sweat 10.82

Table 5: Collocations concerning hurt and irritation to sensory organs

4.2 Interaction with taste sense

Except for the relieving effect of sweetness on the burning sensation produced by capsaicin as mentioned earlier, spicy and numbing can also affect tastes. Our data show that (1) the spicy and numbing flavours usually make it harder for diners to perceive other tastes, and (2) display a close relation with bitterness in the later stage of dining. Both can be supported by studies in neuroscience and pharmacology.

When we get the collocations of 味觉 'taste', the following words appear: 刺激 'to irritate' 13, 丧失 'to lose' 11.99, 失灵 'to malfunction' 11.83, 冲击 'to strike' 11.19, 失去 'to lose' 10.82, which suggests that the irritation of spicy and numbing will make diners cannot feel other tastes well. This is consistent with the finding that chilli pungency may reduce the taste intensity of foods into which it is incorporated (Prescott & Stevenson, 1995). In addition, according to Rong *et al.* (2016), Sichuan pepper contains the anaesthetic constituents, which can also reduce the taste intensity.

Collocations in Table 6 imply another effect of spiciness and numbness on tastes. The spicy and numbing hot pot is very likely to turn bitter after boiling for some time. Previous research in neuroscience may also provide an explanation. Green & Schullery (2003) claim that capsaicin is capable of stimulating a subset of taste neurons that respond to bitter substances, and when applied to small areas of the tongue, capsaicin can produce a bitter taste as well as sensory irritation. Actually, some people experience capsaicin as a moderately intense bitter taste (Mouritsen & Styrbæk, 2017, p.21).

苦 bitter	煮到(后期) boil to (later) 9.71, 吃到(后面) eat to (later) 8.05, (越)煮(越) (the more) boil 7.52, 时间 time 7.27
发苦 turn bitter	后面 later 9.31

Table 5: Collocations with bitter taste

4.3 Effect on smell

Spicy and numbing are not olfactory senses, but daily experience tells us that we can 'smell' them, especially the spicy flavour, which often irritates the nose and cause people to sneeze or cough. There is evidence in our data showing that spicy and numbing can influence smell - their fragrance (香味) can be 'smelt' (闻到), pervade (弥漫) in the air (空气), cover (掩盖) other smell, or cause irritation (刺激 and 呛) to olfactory organ (as shown in Table 6).

闻到 smell	就咳咳咳 then cough 11, 火锅味 hot pot aroma 10.09, 海椒 chilli pepper 9.91, 辣椒味 chilli pepper aroma 9.35, 香辣 fragrant and spicy 9.14, 辣味 spicy taste 8.33
气息 odour	花椒 Sichuan pepper 11.19
辣味 spicy taste	掩盖 cover 8.93, 闻到 smell 8.33, 香 fragrant 8.24
麻 numbing	香味 fragrance 8.24
辣椒 chilli pepper	气呛 irritating 8.98, 弥漫 pervade 8.46
花椒 Sichuan pepper	很香 very fragrant 10.27, 弥漫 pervade 10.14
呛 irritate	空气 air 10.91, 火锅味 hot pot aroma 10.41
刺激 irritate	闻到 smell 9.14

Table 6: Collocations concerning the effect of spicy and numbing on smell

4.4 Relation with mouthfeel

Mouritsen & Styrbæk (2017) state that our understanding of the interplay between chemical sensory impressions and mouthfeel is more limited than the understanding of how sight, hearing, and somatosensory impressions are integrated. 'Mouthfeel' is the central element of the total flavour experience (Mouritsen & Styrbæk, 2017), therefore, it would be of some value if we could acquire certain findings on the interaction of 'spicy' and 'numbing' with mouthfeel. However, 'spicy' and 'numbing' have a very limited relation with mouthfeel according to our data. Words collocated with 口感 'mouthfeel' can be found in the corpus, such as (Q) 弹 'bouncy', 爽脆 'refreshing and crispy/crunchy', 嫩滑 'tender and smooth', etc., but they only refer to the texture of foods in the pot. Only a few words describing mouthfeel could be identified in the collocations with spicy and numbing, for example, 麻 'numbing' can coexist with 厚重 'thick and heavy' 8.82 and 干 'dry' 7.76; while 辣 'spicy' can collocate with 不燥 'not dry' 9.44 and 干 'dry'[6] 8.66.

5 Conclusion

Due to the time-honoured culture originated from 五味 'five tastes', Chinese people have a deep-rooted belief that 'spicy' and 'numbing' are two of the basic tastes. However, the usage of Chinese language concerning spicy and numbing food demonstrates that Chinese people actually perceive such flavours as the non-taste chemesthesis. Being non-tastes, spicy and numbing do interact with taste and smell to some extent, but only have a limited relation with mouthfeel.

An explanation from synaesthesia studies can be provided to account for the divergence of 'spicy' and 'numbing' being deemed tastes while perceived as chemesthesis. Linguistic synaesthesia is a metaphorical process of transfer from one sensory modality (source) to a different one (target). A perceptual experience related to one sense is described by lexical means usually associated to a different sense (Strik Lievers & Huang, 2016). It is thus possible that in our case of 'spicy' and 'numbing', tastes and chemesthesis may exhibit such a synaesthetic relation.

Chemesthesis, as we mentioned previously, is chemical sensitivity derives from nerve fibres of touch, temperature, and pain, and should be classified as touch in the Aristotelian five-sense system (Strik Lievers & Huang, 2016; Zhao, Xiong & Huang, in press). Zhao & Huang (2018), Zhao, Huang & Long (in press), Zhao, Xiong & Huang (in press) claim that 辣 'spicy', together with 苦 'bitter' and 酸 'sour', demonstrate the transfer from taste to touch (in the five-sense system)[7], as in 感觉眼辣手冷 'feeling burning pain in eyes and cold in hands', 苦寒 'bitter cold', 觉得鼻子一酸 'feeling sore in the nose'. Some findings in our study can fit exactly into this model of synaesthesia. Being two of the basic tastes in Chinese culture, 'spicy' and 'numbing', via synaesthesia, can collocate with 'hurt' and 'irritation' of the tactile sense, as shown in section 3.1 and 4.1. They also have extended meanings related to physical irritation and numbness, as discussed in section 3.4. It is most likely that the neurophysiological properties of 'spicy' and 'numbing' as chemesthesis are the bases of such synaesthesia.

Several limitations to this study need to be acknowledged. First, the relations, especially the differences in spicy and numbing perceived by Chinese people are rarely looked into. This is due to the characteristics of our data source. The food types we choose are considered to contain the most concentrated spicy and numbing flavour, thus such two flavours must be very closely interrelated in

[6] More precisely, here 干 and 不燥 mean '(not) causing the effect of dryness'. According to Filingeri *et al.* (2014), humans are not provided with specific skin receptors for sensing wetness and humidity, and wetness perception is intertwined with the ability to sense cold temperature and tactile sensations. Therefore, 干/燥 'dry' may also belong to chemesthesis, and refer to a special condition of mucous membranes, where with some humidity is the norm. In that case, 厚重 would be the only mouthfeel word in our data that collocates with spicy and numbing.

[7] In determining the basic perception lexemes of words, previous studies adopt a combination of introspection and linguistic literature. For the identification of syneasthesia in Chinese, the criteria are mainly based on the abundant classic texts, highly reliable ancient and modern dictionaries, and the radicals of most Chinese characters (Strik Lievers & Huang, 2016; Zhao, Xiong & Huang, in press).

the corpus. In fact, as mentioned by Dunlop (2008), Sichuan pepper is typically used in conjunction with the chillies. The collocations of 麻 'numbing' in Figure 1 has clearly displayed its relation with 辣味 'spicy taste' 12.41 and 辣 'spicy' 9.95.

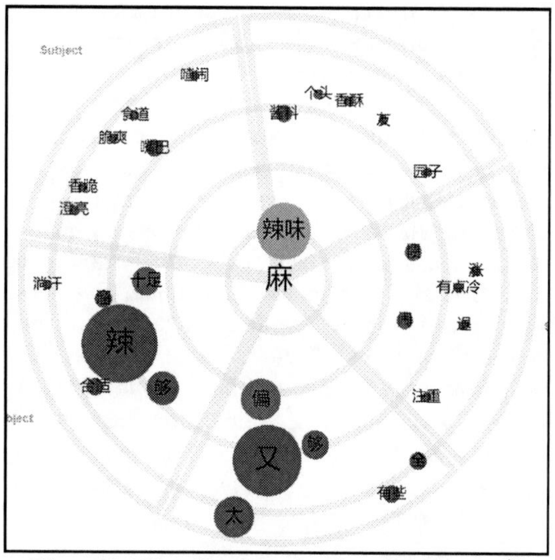

Figure 1: Visualisation of collocations with 麻 'numbing' in the *Sketch Engine*

Second, spicy and numbing are proved to be related to senses of touch, pain and temperature, but the thermal aspect of chemesthesis can hardly be discussed in this study. Some collocations with words related to high temperature were found, such as 热 *re* 'hot', nevertheless, the hot pot and skewer hot pot are both boiling hot, so it is difficult to figure out if the hot feeling is caused by chemesthesis or the hot broth. A possible study in the future will be on the linguistic uses when people are having spicy and numbing cold dishes.

References

Bryant, Bruce P., & Mezine, Igor. (1999). Alkylamides that produce tingling paresthesia activate tactile and thermal trigeminal neurons. *Brain Research*, *842* (2), 452-460.

Duan, Yucai. (1815). *ShuoWenJieZi Zhu* [Annotations to ShuoWenJieZi].Retrieved from https://ctext.org/zh

Dunlop, Fuchsia. (2008). *Shark's fin and Sichuan pepper: A sweet-sour memoir of eating in China*. New York & London: W. W. Norton & Company.

Filingeri, Davide, Fournet, Damien, Hodder, Simon, & Havenith, George. (2014). Why wet feels wet? A neurophysiological model of human cutaneous wetness sensitivity. *Journal of Neurophysiology*, *112* (6), 1457-1469.

Green, Barry G. (1996). Chemesthesis: pungency as a component of flavor. *Trends in Food Science & Technology*, *7* (12), 415-420.

Green, Barry G. (2016). Introduction: what is chemesthesis? In Shane T. McDonald *et al.* (eds.), *Chemesthesis: Chemical touch in food and eating* (pp. 1-7). Chichester, West Sussex: Wiley Blackwell.

Green, Barry G., & Schullery, Matthew T. (2003). Stimulation of bitterness by capsaicin and menthol: differences between lingual areas innervated by the glossopharyngeal and chorda tympani nerves. *Chemical Senses*, *28* (1), 45-55.

Hagura, Nobuhiro, Barber, Harry, & Haggard, Patrick. (2013). Food vibrations: Asian spice sets lips trembling. *Proceedings of the Royal Society B*, *280* (1770), 1-6.

Kilgarriff, Adam, Baisa, Vít, Bušta, Jan, Jakubíček, Miloš, Kovář, Vojtěch, Michelfeit, Jan,...Suchomel, Vít. (2014). The Sketch Engine: Ten years on. *Lexicography*, *1*, 7-36.

Lü, Buwei. (247-239 B.C.). *Lüshi Chunqiu* [Master Lü's Spring and Autumn Annals]. Retrieved from https://ctext.org/zh

Mouritsen, Ole G., & Styrbæk, Klavs. (2014). *Umami: Unlocking the secrets of the fifth taste*. New York, NY & Chichester, West Sussex: Columbia University Press.

Mouritsen, Ole G., & Styrbæk, Klavs. (2017). *Mouthfeel: How texture makes taste*. New York, NY & Chichester, West Sussex: Columbia University Press.

Parker, George H. (1912). The relations of smell, taste, and the common chemical sense in vertebrates. *Journal of the Academy of Natural Sciences of Philadelphia*, *15*, 221-234.

Prescott, John, & Stevenson, Richard J. (1995). Pungency in food perception and preference. *Food Reviews International*, *11* (4), 665-698.

Rakova, Marina. (2003). *The extent of the literal: Metaphor, polysemy and theories of concepts*. Basingstoke, Hampshire & New York, NY: Palgrave MacMillan.

Rong, Rong, Cui, Mei-Yu, Zhang, Qi-Li, Zhang, Mei-Yan, Yu, Yu-Ming, Zhou, Xian-Ying,...Zhao, Yun-Li. (2016). Anesthetic constituents of *Zanthoxylum bungeanum* Maxim.: A pharmacokinetic study. *Journal of Separation Science*, *39* (14), 2728-2735.

Strik Lievers, Francesca, & Huang, Chu-Ren. (2016). A lexicon of perception for the identification of synaesthetic metaphors in corpora. *Proceedings of the 10th Language Resources and Evaluation Conference (LREC 2016)*, 4032-4036.

Zhao, Qingqing, & Huang, Chu-Ren. (2018) Xiandai Hanyu tonggan yinyu de yingshe moxing yu zhiyue jizhi [Mapping models and underlying mechanisms of synaesthetic metaphors in Mandarin]. *Language Teaching and Linguistic Studies*, (1), 44-55.

Zhao, Qingqing, Huang, Chu-Ren, & Long, Yunfei. (in press). Synaesthesia in Chinese: A corpus-based study on gustatory adjectives in Mandarin. *Linguistics*.

Zhao, Qingqing, Xiong, Jiajuan, & Huang, Chu-Ren. (in press). Tonggan yinyu yu renzhi: Tonggan xianxiang zai Hanyu zhong de xitongxing biaoxian yu yuyanxue jiazhi [Linguistic synaesthesia, metaphor and cognition: The systematicity and significance of linguistic synaesthesia in Chinese]. *Zhongguo Yuwen*.

Zhao, Rongguang. (2003). *Zhongguo yinshi wenhua gailun* [An introduction to Chinese dietetic culture]. Beijing: Higher Education Press.

Zhao, Rongguang. (2006). *Zhongguo yinshi wenhua shi* [The history of Chinese dietetic culture]. Shanghai: Shanghai People's Publishing House.

Flavor Wheel Terminology and Challenges in Translation --Focusing on English and Japanese Vocabulary for Wine, Sake and Soy sauce --

Nami Fukutome
Graduate School of Japanese Applied Linguistics , Waseda University, 1-104 Nishiwaseda, Shinjuku-ku, Tokyo 169-0051 Japan
namifukutome@akane.waseda.jp

Yasunari Harada
Faculty of Law, Waseda University
1-6-1 Nishi-Waseda, Shinjuku-ku, Tokyo 169-8050, Japan
harada@waseda.jp

Abstract

This report highlights the delicate and complicated issues of English and Japanese translation of terms that express the flavor and aroma characteristics of foods/drinks. First, we compared English and Japanese terms on the aroma wheel for wine, and flavor wheels for sake and soy sauce. Our analysis focused on whether the subjects denoted by the Japanese and English terms representing taste, aroma and flavor are the same in the contexts of Japan and UK / US – regions with different food cultures; if there is the possibility of a discrepancy; and where there are differences, what kind of measures are taken to share the true meaning of the term. Our research enabled us to classify the subjects denoted by terms for aroma and taste into four categories: 1) subjects that are more or less the same in the original language as in the translation (further classified by ease of access); 2) subjects for which a translation exists but may carry a different meaning; 3) subjects for which the translation deviates from the original; and 4) subjects for which no translation exists and are therefore shown in the original language.

We then recognized that in order to understand characteristic foods and drinks, which are intricately linked with the identity of each region, it is not sufficient to provide literal translation; it is important to be sensitive to similarities and differences in both concrete objects and general concepts across regions in order to accurately capture the meaning denoted by the terms for them in the original and translated forms.

1 Introduction

The first author of this paper has long worked in the field of food science. She lived in France for one year conducting research on French gastronomy and she has been studying cooking and food culture in Japan for many years. When she studied wine, she was puzzled by many of the materials mentioned on the aroma wheel as she had never eaten them in Japan, and some of those were hard to gain first-hand experience of even in France. Ultimately, she came to the conclusion that it is important not only to actually taste a lot of wine, but also to taste a lot of foods/drinks other than wine and accumulate experiences of all sorts of aromas in ordinary life. In short, in order to understand sensory expressions, the key is to build a portfolio of real experiences, using all five senses. An accumulation of real taste and smell experiences builds understanding of the unique characteristics of previously unknown foods/drinks from different cultures and helps us become more perceptive about how they are received in the original cultural sphere. This can be compared to saying that a deep appreciation and comprehension of foreign literature requires not only understanding of that foreign language, but also exposure to numerous literary works in one's own mother tongue and other languages, taking time to carefully understand the meanings and concepts behind the words in the process.

In this study, we analyzed terms in the English aroma wheel for wine, widely recognized in Western countries, and for comparison, we also analyzed the flavor wheel for sake. In addition, we looked at the flavor wheel for soy sauce, an original Japanese seasoning, to ascertain the difficulty of translating terminology created in Japanese on the basis of Japanese food culture. The purpose of this research is to clarify the delicate and complicated issues found in translating terms that describe the characteristics of foods/drinks with regards to flavor and aroma in English and Japanese. It also raises various general issues found in language translation.

2 Method

We analyzed three aroma wheel / flavor wheels – those for wine, sake, and soy sauce – each with notation in both English and Japanese.

Aromaster, the Master Sommelier Wine Aroma Wheel * 1) was used for wine. In addition to being widely recognized as one of the highest quality wine aroma wheels, it is available in multiple languages. This time, we examined it by matching English and Japanese terminology on the wheel. For examination in the sake field, we used the Sake flavor wheel made by the National Research Institute of Brewing (NRIB) * 2), 3). It is the only flavor wheel available for sake created by a public agency. As for soy sauce, we used the flavor wheel * 4), 5) made by Kikkoman, the world's largest soy sauce manufacturer. It was the first aroma/flavor wheel of its kind for soy sauce. It was first produced in English covering pasteurized soy sauce varieties most commonly consumed outside Japan. The Japanese version was then created by adding characteristics of soy sauce sold in Japan, including raw (unpasteurized) soy sauce which is increasingly popular in Japan. Therefore, this flavor wheel for soy sauce was prepared separately in Japanese and English, and therefore may, strictly speaking, not be a translation. However, there are many common terms which are thought to have a corresponding relationship.

Aromaster's aroma wheel lists 88 words for aromas found in wine. In this study, we classified the English and Japanese equivalents for those 88 words. The sake flavor wheel cites 42 words and each has an English translation. In this study, we classified the correspondence between the 42 words in English and Japanese. The English version of Kikkoman's flavor wheel organizes 88 distinctive aromas / tastes / flavors / textures, of which 74 characteristics are common to Japanese soy sauce. Excluding duplications, the Japanese version contains a total of 91 terms after accounting for the characteristics of products sold exclusively in Japan, including raw (unpasteurized) soy sauce. * 5) Therefore, for the purposes of this study, we classified only the 74 words considered to express features exhibited by products both overseas and in Japan. In the aroma wheels used in this study, whereas wine terms only refer to aroma, sake terms cover both aroma and flavor, and soy sauce terms cover aroma, flavor and texture. Since the purpose of this research is to classify correspondence of each translation within a single wheel rather than comparing the three, we examined each wheel in its entirety.

Issues that need to be considered in the classification process are as follows. The terms included in the aroma / flavor wheels are sensory evaluation terms used to assess the aromas and flavors of foods and drinks. The evaluator needs to know and remember the aromas and flavors that the terms imply, so that they can use those terms as an evaluation measure. The terms included in aroma and flavor wheels are mostly the names of specific foods and objects found in daily life. Therefore, through the food items and other objects, you get a sense of the characteristic aromas or flavors contained therein and come to recognize and associate them with names for things, which you are then able to memorize.

For example, although the main substance that constitutes the scent of banana is isoamyl acetate, people associate other trace ingredients and sense a "banana-ish" or "banana-like" aroma. The aromas of foods and other subjects shown on the flavor wheel indicate the characteristic and representative aromas of the most typical form of such an item. Wine contains various fragrance substances, but the delicately balanced individual fragrance substances can be detected, and you can sense an array of "something-like"/"something-ish" fragrances. Sometimes the terms in the flavor wheel refer to the name of the actual substance that gives the sense of a certain aroma or flavor. For example, acetic acid is the main substance in vinegar and a substance that makes you sense sourness. Among the flavor wheels, some use the term "vinegar" while others use "acetic acid", showing different levels of detail in terms of indicating sourness.

As described above, different levels of nomenclature are mixed with various metaphorical expressions and the terms for subjects range from generic names to unique substance names. How can we classify these terms of flavor and aroma? In this study, we tried to classify these terms based on the subjects denoted in flavor/aroma wheels and the level of accessibility to those items.

3 Result 1: Classification of Terms Based on Translation Interpretations

We classified the terms based on interpretations of translation from Japanese to English and from Japanese to English, and what kind of aroma or flavor the respective terms actually denote. This resulted in four broad categories: 1) subjects that are more or less the same in the original language as in the translation (further classified by ease of access); 2) subjects for which a translation exists but may carry a different meaning; 3) subjects for which the translation deviates from the original; and 4) subjects for which no translation exists and are therefore shown in the original language (Table1).

Even within category 1), with regards to different food cultures, the biggest difference was whether a specific item was readily accessible in the other region. If the item used to convey the characteristic flavor and aroma is readily available, then it is easy to understand and relate to, but if it is not available then it is hard to understand.

Table1. Categories of Subjects Found in Flvor /Aroma Wheels

	Wine	Sake	Soy sauce
1) Same in both English and Japanese	67	24	41
easy to access	45	16	29
not easy to access	22	8	12
2) Possibly different meaning	17	10	16
3) Deviation from original meaning	3	3	14
4) No translation exists	1	5	3
Total	88	42	74

Table 2. Terms Same in Both English and Japanese – Wine, Sake and Soy Sauce –

Wine Japanese/English
easy to access
remon/lemon, raimu/lime, gurepu-furutu/grapefruit, Yonashi/pear, ringo/apple, meron/melon, painappuru/pineapple, passhon-furutu/passion fruit, raichi/lychee, dorai-apurikotto/dry apricot, orenji-no-kawa/orange peel, banana/banana, razu-beri/raspberry, ichigo/strawberry, puramu/plum, dorai-furutu/prune, jasumin/jasmine, bara/rose, rabenda/lavender, fenneru/fennel, tomato/tomato, diru/dill, taimu/thyme, minto/mint, bei-rifu/bay leaf, toyu/kerosene, bata/butter, kyarameru/caramel, chokoreto/chocolate, tosuto/toast, banira/vanilla, kuro-kosho/pepper, shinamon/cinnamon, natsumegu/nutmeg, kurobu/clove, kokonattu/coconut, hezerunattu/hazelnut, amondo/almond, matsu/pine, toryufu/truffle, sheri-shu/sherry, madeira-wain/madeila, binega/vinegar, joko-eki/nail polish remover, tamanegi/onion, suito-kon/sweet corn
not easy to access
oku/oak, guzu-beri/gooseberry, guava/guava, kashisu/blackcurrant, burakku-beri/blackberry, suikazura/honeysuckle, sanzashi/howthorn, orenji-no-hana/orange blossom, bodaiju/linden, akashia/acacia, sumire/violet, kashisu-no-ha/black currant leaf, yukari-no-ha/eucalyplus, youso/iodine, hiuchi-ishi/flint, bekon/bacon, taru/tar, sandaru-wood/sandalwood, marumero-zeri/quince jelly , gurebi/gravy, uma-no-ase/horse sweat
Sake Japanese/English
easy to access
koge-shu/Burnt, jushi-shu/Plastic, arukoru/Alcoholic, nuka/Rice bran, karameru-yo/Caramel, kobo-yo/Yeasty, kabi-shu/Musty, sanmi/Sour, amami/Sweet Aroma, shioaji, emmi/Salty, umami/Umami, nigami/Bitter, shibumi/Astringent, shigeki-mi/Pungent, tansan gas/Carbonation, kinzoku-mi/Metallic
not easy to access
esuteru/Estery, ryukabutsu-yo/Sulfidic, arudehido/Aldelydic, nikko-shu/Light struck, kami-shu, hokori-shu, tsuchi-shu/Papery/Dusty/Earthy, jiasechiru/Diacetyl, san-shu/Rancid/Acetic, kime/Smoothness
Soy sauce Japanese/English
easy to access
daizu/Soybean, sumi/Burnt, piripiri/Prickling , watagashi/Cotton candy, shoku-su/Vinegar, yusei-majikku/Magic marker, shodoku-yaku/Disinfectant, satsumaimo/Sweet potato, tosuto/Toast, daku chokoreto/Dark chocolate, akikan/Tin, tetsu/Iron, oisuta-sosu/Oyster sauce, amami/Sweetness, shio-aji/Saltiness, sanmi/Sourness, nigami/Bitterness, shibumi/Astringent, atoaji-no-amami/Lasting sweetness, atoaji-no-shioaji/Lasting saltiness, atoaji-no-sanmi/Lasting sourness, atoaji-no-nigami/Lasting bitterness, watagashi/Cotton candy, shoku-su/Vinegar, etanoru-shu/Ethanol, daizu/Soybean, satsumaimo/Sweet potato, tosuto/Toast, maku-ga-haru/Coating
not easy to access
etanoru-shu/Ethanol , kombu-dashi/Kelp broth, kome-nuka/Rice-bran, nukadoko/Rice-bran paste, kidaru/Barrel , bokuju/Chinese ink, kachiku-sha/Barn, umami/Umami, atoaji-no-umami/Lasting umami, kombu-dashi/Kelp broth, katsuo-dashi/Bonito broth, shiitake/Shitake

Terms found to be the same in both languages (Category 1) for wine, sake and soy sauce are summarized in Table 2.

4 Result 2: Comparison of Terms for Wine, Sake, and Soy Sauce

Below is a list of corresponding terms classified as having different meanings or having no available translation (Table 3-1, 2, 3).

As shown in Table3-1, of the 88 terms extracted from the wine aroma / flavor wheel, the word from the original language was used for just one term. Bouchonné, the French word meaning "corked" in English, is used as is in the Japanese translation. This seems to be because it in addition to the absence of a corresponding Japanese term, it has become more widely recognized relatively recently in Japan as indicating bad flavor. The problem when translating the aroma / flavor of wine is whether the term translated from the original word into the corresponding Japanese makes Japanese people recall an image identical to that recalled by French, American and English people, for example.

Of the 87 terms given as translations, we found that 67 of them indicated clear and concrete subjects. And of these, about 45 words point to common and familiar subjects for both Japanese and Table3-1. Wine Aroma Wheel Terms Requiring More Attention in Translation westerners, making the aromas easy to imagine and therefore leading to a low likelihood of translation problems. Examples include items like lemon, lime, rose, mint, and chocolate. On the other hand, regarding the remaining 22 words, although there is no translation issue for the terms themselves, there is a possibility that the aroma evoked by that word may be different for Japanese and Westerners, so more attention is required in translation. For example, although it may be possible to imagine actual objects such as gooseberry, guava, cassis, honeysuckle, linden, violet, eucalyptus leaves, it is not easy for ordinary Japanese people to imagine their aromas / flavors, and there is also a possibility that people would imagine a totally different thing.

Table3-1. Wine Aroma/Flavor Wheel Terms Requiring More Attention in Translation

WINE terms Japanese / English		2) Possibly different meaning	3) Deviation from original meaning	4) No translation exists
Aroma				
ao-ringo	green apple	1		
momo	peach	1		
sakurambo	cherry	1		
piman	capsicum		1	
sibafu	cut grass	1		
shida	fern	1		
hoshikusa	hay	1		
kocha	black tea	1		
tabako	tabacco	1		
pan	bread	1		
kohi	coffee	1		
kemuri	smoke	1		
kanzo	liquorice		1	
Himaraya-sugi	cedar		1	
hachimitsu	honey	1		
shoyu	soy sauce	1		
kawa	leather	1		
masshurumu	mushroom	1		
ki-no-koke	tree moss	1		
bushone	corked			1
gomu	rubber	1		
total		17	3	1

Furthermore, for 17 of those 22 words, because the terms are common there is such a variety of aromas / flavors that people may recall that the real intention may not be accurately transmitted. For example, translating green apple directly as ao-ringo may be correct, but the small green apple commonly found in Europe is not distributed in Japan, so it is not clear what Japanese people think of when they hear 'green apples'. There is also a difference between peaches and Japanese white peaches, cherries and sakurambo Japanese cherries. In such cases, there is usually a method of translation that shows the difference by including a place name as in "American cherry", or by adding a color classification or a variety name like "yellow peach".

Next, we present Table 3-2. Of the 42 terms extracted from the Japanese sake aroma / flavor wheel, the original word was used as is for 5 terms: ginjo-ka, koji, hine-ka, namahine-ka, amakara. All of them indicate flavors peculiar to sake, and like bouchonné in wine, it seems recognition of the original word and the flavors associated with it has spread with the increase in sake lovers around the world. There were also three words where the meaning was changed by the translation. If translated directly, "kika" means "flavor of tree", but likely to avoid ambiguity, it has been translated as "Japanese cedar". Also, "notan (shading)", usually an indication of complexity, has been translated as "body"; and "nori-mi", literally "glue flavor", is a special phrase that has been translated as "mouth coating".

One major difference from the aroma wheel for wine is that there are few words in the sake wheel indicating the scent of specific fruits and flowers. In addition to sake not being a drink derived from fruit, this is also thought to be due to the fact that explanations for sake that need to convey fruit and flower aromas/ flavors are often provided by borrowing from wine terminology. Eighteen of the 34 words to which the equivalent term was applied point to objects we considered difficult to imagine as they carry such broad meaning or because they are difficult to recall. "Kajitsu-yo (fruit-like)" is fruity, "hana-yo (flower-like)" is floral, "kinomi-yo (nut-like)" is nutty, but the range of possibilities is so broad that it is unclear whether people will be able to think of the specific flavors the words refer to. Using more specific fruit, flower, or nut names may result in the same kinds of issues faced in the translation of wine flavors.

As for the translation of the soy sauce aroma / flavor wheel, as shown in Table 3-3, among the 74 corresponding terms found in both language wheels, three were the original Japanese, and as many as 14 terms were found to be changed from literal translation. Those using the original language were natto, umeboshi, and koku – expressions of food and flavor peculiar to Japan, and for which the foods themselves are recognized around the world in the original language. On the other hand, examples where the terms were changed in-translation include translating "kokuto (black sug ar)" as "brown sugar" and "shiro-wine (white wine)" as "fruity" . Sugar with low purity is called "black" sugar in Japanese but referred to as "brown" sugar in English-speaking countries. Clearly the literal translation does not work in this case. Brown sugar in the United States has a rather high level of refinement and milder flavor compared to "black" sugar from Okinawa which has low purity and strong flavor. Thus, if you wish to express the strength of the soy sauce aroma more precisely it may be necessary to explain further.

Table3-2. Sake Aroma/Flavor Wheel Terms Requiring More Attention in Translation

***Sake* terms** Japanese / English		2) Possibly different meaning	3) Deviation from original meaning	4) No translation exists
	odor			
ginjo-ka	*Ginjyo-ka*			1
kajitu-yo	Fruity	1		
hana-yo	Floral	1		
kika	Japanese cedar		1	
kusa-yo/ao-shu	Grassy	1		
kinomi-yo	Nutty	1		
koshinryo-yo	Spicy	1		
kokurui-yo	Grainy	1		
koji	*Koji (Fungus)*			1
ama-shu	Sweet Aroma	1		
hine-ka	*Hine-ka*			1
namahine-ka	*Nama hine-ka*			1
gomu-shu	Rubbery	1		
shibo-san	Fatty acid	1		
	Taste			
nori-aji	Mouth coating		1	
ato-aji	Afterfeel	1		
amakara	***Amakara (Dryness)***			1
notan	Body		1	
total		10	3	5

The other example was of the flavor of "white wine" being translated as "fruity" to describe the flavor of soy sauce. More specifically, it is explained as fruity esters and fruity aroma of white wine. If there is a white wine flavor in Japan's original seasoning soy sauce, it is natural for Japanese to associate that with a fruity aroma, but what kind of aromas does the term "white wine" evoke for an American, for example, perhaps less familiar with soy sauce? This is one clear case for mak ing a point of changing a translation taking into account levels of familiarity and experience with the flavors. By the way, "aka-wine (red wine)" flavor is translated just the same as "red wine" and explained as "red wine astringent aroma associated with red wine/skin of red grapes". Compared to white wine fruit aroma, perhaps red wine astringency is more easily associated with soy sauce.

Table3-3. Soy Sauce Aroma/Flavor Wheel Terms Requiring More Attention in Translation

Soy Sauce terms Japanese / English		2) Possibly different meaning	3) Deviation from original meaning	4) No translation exists
Aroma				
mure-ka	Damp	1		
konappoi	Powdery	1		
shigeki-shu	Pungent	1		
kokuto	Brown sugar		1	
shiro-wain	Fruity		1	
yo-shu	Liqueur	1		
aka-wain	Red wine	1		
tsukemono	Pickle		1	
kankitsu	Vinegar	1		
hinoki	Cypress tree		1	
ugai-gusuri	Iodine		1	
beihan	Rice		1	
sumi	Burnt		1	
kohi-no-degarashi	Coffee grounds		1	
bekon	Smoked food		1	
kinoko	Mushroom	1		
iso	Fish		1	
kombu	Briny	1		
sakana	Seaweed	1		
abura	Oily	1		
mame-miso	Bean paste		1	
natto	*Natto*			1
kocha	Black tea	1		
Taste				
koku	*Koku*			1
Flavor				
kokuto	Brown sugar		1	
tsukemono	Pickle		1	
kankitsu	Citrus	1		
umeboshi	*Umeboshi*			1
ugai-gusuri	Iodine		1	
maitake	Mushroom	1		
sashimi	Fish	1		
kombu	Seaweed	1		
Texture				
toromi	Viscous	1		
total		16	14	3

5 Conclusion

In the translation of wine, sake, and soy sauce flavor wheels, we found that subjects denoted with literal translations can be difficult to imagine, possibly leading to recall of different aromas. In order to avoid such issues, it may be wise to use the original word in the source language as is, and for the detail to be understood subsequently as familiarity with the food/drink grows. Also, it may be easier to imagine certain aromas / flavors by replacing the term with a different word instead of translating it directly, though this then raises the possible issue that the subject imagined is not identical to the subject denoted by the original term. In such cases, it would be necessary to confirm through processes such as actual tasting whether the corresponding terms from the two languages represent the same meaning in each society.

This research focused on English-Japanese translation equivalents in flavor and aroma wheels for foods and drinks. In translating the "language of food," the terminology only conveys part of the picture and it became clear that it is necessary to undertake a confirmation process to avoid discrepancies between the terms used and the flavors actually experienced. For that reason, individuals must engage in shared taste experiences in order to truly understand and redefine the meaning of the words. We would argue that this need to share the meaning of words through such experiences is relevant to the translation of all kinds of language pairs.

References

1) Aromaster, The Master Sommelier Wine Aroma Wheel, http://www.aromaster.com/ (accessed June 30, 2018).
2) National Research Institute of Brewing (NRIB), Sake Terms trial ver.4, revised 2018/3/30, https://www.nrib.go.jp/sake/pdf/nrib_st_ver4.pdf (accessed September 15, 2018).
3) Utsunomiya, H., Isogai, A., Iwata, H., & Nakano, S., 2006, Flavor Terminology and Reference Standards for Sensory Analysis of *Sake*, Report of the Research Institute of Brewing, 178:45-52
4) Imamura, M., 2016. Descriptive Terminology for the Sensory Evaluation of Soy Sauce, Journal of Sensory Studies, 31(5):393-407
5) Imamura, M., & Katayama, H., 2017, Sensory Differences between Commercialized Raw (unheated)- and Heated-Soy Sauces: Organization of Sensory Attributes to Evaluate Japanese Soy Sauce, Nippon Shokuhin Kagaku Kagaku Kaishi, 64(7), 343-354

Conceptual Metaphorical Extensions of 'Eat' and 'Drink' in English and Korean: A Usage-based Approach

Jong-Bok Kim
Kyung Hee University
jongbok@khu.ac.kr

Jungsoo Kim
Kyung Hee University
jungsookim@khu.ac.kr

Rok Sim
Kyung Hee University
simrok89@khu.ac.kr

Abstract

This paper discusses conceptual metaphorical extensions with 'eat' and 'drink' in two typologically different languages, English and Korean. We first investigate their uses in attested data and explore their grammatical properties as well as metaphorical uses. The two languages display quite similar behavior in terms of the metaphorical extensions of the two verbs, but at the same time show differences in several respects. The paper suggests that the similarities may have to do with the fact that such ingestive events/acts involve several facets in common while the differences are caused by linguistic as well as cultural differences.

1 Introduction

Eating food and drinking liquids represent universal practices amongst humans (Newman, 1997, 2009; Wierzbicka, 2009; Naess, 2009). The two verbs 'eat' and 'drink' are conceptually similar in that both are closely related to the intake of food and beverages into the mouth and digestive tract (Newman, 2009), as exemplified in the following:[1]

(1) a. You're not supposed to eat the bacon. (COCA, 1998, Spoken)

b. Lindsay would drink beer and shoot pool with her brother-in-law. (COCA, 1992, Fiction)

As pointed out by Newman (2009), the two verbs, however, differ in terms of Active Zone and Force Dynamics. In other words, eating involves mouth, teeth, tongue, and palate, while drinking does not require any of these active zone components. In addition, eating includes forceful crushing and biting of food whereas drinking accompanis no change to liquid.

This paper first discusses basic semantic/pragmatic properties of ingestive verbs, focusing mainly on 'eat' and 'drink' in English and Korean. The paper then investigates conceptual metaphorical extensions we find with these ingestive verbs in the two languages. In doing so, we search authentic corpus data to check real uses of 'eat' and 'drink' in literal as well as metaphorical sense. The paper then discusses a contrastive analysis of the conceptual metaphorical uses of 'eat' and 'drink' while looking into the similarities as well as differences.

2 Conceptual metaphorical uses of *eat* and *drink* in English

2.1 Basic properties

In English, *eat* and *drink* can be used as transitive as well as intransitive verbs, as illustrated below:

(2) a. You should stop at every one and eat a banana and drink some Gatorade. (COCA, 2010, News)

b. I would drink lots of water before leaving for the hospital. (COCA, 2010, Fiction)

(3) a. The same event of a dog eating hungrily from the bowl can be equally well described with these two verbs. (COCA, 2010, Academic)

[1] COCA: Corpus of Contemporary American English

32nd Pacific Asia Conference on Language, Information and Computation
The 25th Joint Workshop on Linguistics and Language Processing
Hong Kong, 1-3 December 2018

b. On Sunday, Grandpa never drank, but he was always hung-over. (COCA, 1991, Fiction)

Transitive uses of these verbs may conceptualize an interactive activity of the subject consumer with the food or drink. On the other hand, intransitive uses of these verbs seem to focus on encoding the experience of the consumer: the sensation of taste, satisfaction, pleasure, or displeasure.

The basic lexical semantics of ingestive verbs in English include facets such as intake, mastication, and ingestion as described in the following table (Newman, 2009; Yamaguchi, 2009; Song, 2009; Hook and Pardeshi, 2009):

Facets	Verbs	Process
INTAKE	*eat, taste* *devour, swallow*	Some solid/liquid-like substance is taken into the mouth
	drink, suck	Some liquid-like substance is taken into the mouth
MASTICATION	*chew, bite*	Mastication of the food takes place, involving the teeth, tongue, and the roof of the mouth
INGESTION	*ingest, digest*	The food undergoes quite drastic transformations

As can be seen here, the simple intake facet is the primary meaning part of ingestive verbs like *eat, devour, drink,* and *suck*, whereas the mastication facet is emphasized in ingestive verbs like *chew* and *bite*. Meanwhile, the ingestion facet is a pivotal part in ingestive verbs such as *ingest* and *digest*. This does not mean that each ingestive verb involves only one meaning facet. Metaphorical uses are extended from such basic conceptual meanings described above.

2.2 Methodology

In order to investigate authentic uses of the two ingestive verbs *eat* and *drink* in English, we have searched the COCA (Corpus of Contemporary American English), the largest freely available online corpus of American English. The COCA consists of 560 million words of text from 1990 to 2017 and it is a balanced corpus with a variety of registers including spoken and written data.[2]

2.3 Conceptual metaphorical extensions of *drink*

One salient conceptual metaphor with *drink* in English is DRINKING IS PLEASANT INHALING as in (4):

(4) a. She sat down in the car with the door open, drinking the fresh air. (COCA, 1997, Fiction)

b. When I hugged her, I drank in her smells: gardenia perfume, face powder, and hair spray. (COCA, 2000, Fiction)

Although drinking literally involves intake of some liquid substance, this is metaphorically extended to gaseous substances such as *air, smell, scent, perfume, aroma, wind*, etc. Sometimes, it combines with a particle *in* as in (4b) and the event typically involves a pleasant experience as we can see the nouns *drink* occurs with.

This type of pleasant experience triggered by *drink* can be further extended to other senses such as seeing, listening, and even touching.

(5) a. And soon his eyes had drunk her beauty up. (COCA, 1992, Fiction)

b. He relaxed into warmth and unaccustomed security, drinking Christmas music from Galway Girl's radio with his strong tea. (COCA, 1994, Fiction)

c. She would drink his kisses as his hands moved over her body, squeezing and stroking. (COCA, 2008, Fiction)

In these examples, *drink* does not mean consuming a liquid substance; rather, it refers to a pleasant sensing event other than drinking in its literal sense.

Another conceptual metaphor with *drink* is DRINKING IS CONSUMING RESOURCES.

(6) a. Copters and private jets drank fuel. (COCA, 2006, Fiction)

b. On top of that, my crane's down there drinking diesel like a drunk sailor, and I'm up here talking to you. (COCA, 2012, Fiction)

c. That SUV just drinks gas. (COCA, 2012, Fiction)

In these examples, the agent is not a human entity; however, the verb *drink* is metaphorically used in that the agent consumes a liquid or gaseous resource to operate in a similar manner to human being needing to drink water to live.

[2] COCA is available at: `https://corpus.byu.edu/coca/`

2.4 Conceptual metaphorical extensions of *eat*

The English word *eat* has more conceptual metaphor types than *drink*. One noticeable metaphor with *eat* observed from the corpus data is EATING IS CONSUMING RESOURCES:

(7) a. His old car was eating up the gas. (COCA, 1996, Fiction)

b. Credit card processing fees eat up more than 5 cents per gallon. (COCA, 2005, News)

c. All right, Hannity, stop eating up my time. (COCA, 2017, Spoken)

In these examples, what is consumed is some type of resource such as gas, money, and even time, regardless of whether the agent is an animate or inanimate entity. Note here that this conceptual metaphor involves the particle *up* in many cases and this is because in general eating is a telic event while drinking is an atelic event (Newman, 2009, Naess, 2009). Notice also that this conceptual metaphor is similar to DRINKING IS CONSUMING RESOURCES; however, this one has wider coverage of the consumed objects.

Another conceptual metaphor with *eat* involves acquiring possession:

(8) a. In 1986, Toyota opened its first American factory. Honda, Nissan, BMW, Mercedes-Benz, Hyundai, and others followed. Relentlessly, they ate into GM's market share. (COCA, 2011, Academic)

b. The machine might eat your card. (COCA, 2012, Fiction)

c. A few customer complaints – the dryer ate my money, rinse cycle's not long enough, that kind of thing. (COCA, 2000, Fiction)

This conceptual metaphor EATING IS ACQUIRING POSSESSION is closely related to the internalization facet of the eating process and it often has a negative connotation.

An additional crucial conceptual metaphor with *eat* concerns destroying as in (9):

(9) a. The Jorissens saw the fire eat up a neighbor's house. (COCA, 2000, Fiction)

b. Sea salt is eating away this rock. (COCA, 2012, Academic)

c. Cancer doesn't just eat at your body; it also attacks you emotionally and psychologically. (COCA, 2002, Magazine)

d. Social inequity eats at public morale. (COCA, 1997, Academic)

In these examples of EATING IS DESTROYING, the agent has an effect in such a way that the object undergoes some kind of concrete or abstract destruction and it usually contains a particle such as *up, away, at,* and *into*.

Lastly, EATING IS FULFILLING BASIC NATURAL DESIRES is a conceptual metaphor whose examples are also frequently found in the corpus:

(10) a. You want to eat, drink, have sex, procreate. That's your basic instincts. And so those little girls are so absolutely beautiful that you're saying, "You know, you're a doll. You're candy. I want to eat you. I want to eat you." Is it, "Do I want to eat you, or do I want to have sex with you?" (COCA, 2006, Spoken)

b. "I would eat that girl's ass." There were enough people within earshot. Odds were someone heard. And if someone heard, they were sure to report the comment to the Davenports. (COCA, 2015, Fiction)

This conceptual metaphor is closely related to sexual activity and in examples involving this metaphor, the object can be a human entity or a human's body part. This conceptual metaphor is assumed to be extended from the "natural desire" and "pleasant activity" facets of the eating process.

3 Conceptual metaphorical uses of *mek-* 'eat' and *masi-* 'drink' in Korean

In this section, we examine basic grammatical and metaphorical uses of *mek-* 'eat' and *masi-* 'drink' in Korean, making use of corpus data. In doing so, we make comparisons with English conceptual metaphors with *eat* and *drink* discussed in the previous section.

3.1 Basic properties

Both *mek-* 'eat' and *masi-* 'drink' verbs in Korean typically occur in the transitive construction (Song, 2009; Lee, 2002, 2012). Intransitive uses are possible, encoding the generic activities of eating and drinking, as shown below:

(11) mek-ko masi-ko nol-ca.
eat-and drink-and play-SUG

'Let's eat, drink and play.'

Similar to English, multifacets of ingestive verbs in Korean can be represented as in the following table:

Facets	Verbs	Process
INTAKE	*mek-* 'eat', *maspo-* 'taste', *chyemek-* 'devour', *samkhi-* 'swallow'	Some solid/liquid-like substance is taken into the mouth
	masi- 'drink', *ppal-* 'suck'	Some liquid-like substance is taken into the mouth
MASTICATION	*ssip-* 'chew, bite'	Mastication of the food takes place, involving the teeth, tongue, and the roof of the mouth
INGESTION	*sepchwiha-* 'ingest', *sohwaha-* 'digest'	The food undergoes quite drastic transformations

Just like English, Korean ingestive verbs have salient facets of the eating/drinking process such as intake, mastication, ingestion, etc., and conceptual metaphors are related to such conceptual meaning components.

One thing to note at this point is that unlike English, in Korean *mek-* 'eat' is a hypernym of *masi-* 'drink' (Song, 2009). That is, in literal uses the verb *masi-* 'drink' can be replaced by *mek-* 'eat', but the reverse is not possible.

(12) a. ku ai-ka wuyu-lul
the child-NOM milk-ACC
masi/mek-ess-e.
drink/eat-PST-DECL

'(lit.) The child drank/ate milk.'

b. ku ai-ka phiza-lul
the child-NOM pizza-ACC
mek/*masi-ess-e.
eat/drink-PST-DECL

'(lit.) The child ate/*drank pizza.'

As can be seen in (12a), *masi-* 'drink' as well as *mek-* can take a liquid substance *milk* as their object; however, as in (12b) only the latter can occur with a solid food entity like *pizza*. In this regard, *mek-* 'eat' is a hypernym of *masi-* 'drink' in Korean.

3.2 Methodology

In order to explore authentic uses of the tow ingestive verbs *mek-* 'eat' and *masi-* 'drink' in Korean, we used the Sejong corpus as the main corpus source.[3] The corpus consists of around 37 million ejels with contemporary Korean data mainly from written material (approximately 36 million ejels for the written data; fewer than 1 million ejels for the spoken data).[4] For the description reflecting uses of *mek-* 'eat' and *masi-* 'drink' fully, we also used data from other materials including web pages and dictionaries.

3.3 Conceptual metaphorical extensions of *masi-* 'drink'

The most common conceptual metaphor with *masi-* 'drink' is DRINKING IS INHALING, as exemplified below:

(13) a. salam-tul-un yenki naymsay cawukhan
peron-PL-TOP smoke smell thick
kongki-lul masy-eya hay-ss-ta.
air-ACC drink-CONN must-PST-DECL

'People had to drink the air thick with smell of smoke. (Sejong Corpus, 1998, Book)

b. i smoku-lul masi-myen am-uy
this smog-ACC drink-if cancer-GEN
wenin-i toy-ko, ...
cause-NOM become-and

'If you drink this smog, it causes cancer and ... (Sejong Corpus, 2003, Book)

Most of the metaphorical examples of *masi-* 'drink' extracted from the Sejong corpus fall into this type. This conceptual metaphor involves nouns such as *kongki* 'air', *kas* 'gas', *naymsay* 'smell', *sanso* 'oxygen', *yenki* 'smoke', *smok* 'smog', *pond* 'gas from glue', and *palam* 'wind'. Note that unlike English this conceptual metaphor does not have positive semantic prosody in that the verb occurs with positive as well as negative nouns.

Observe then that this type of conceptual metaphor with *masi-* 'drink' can be further extended

[3]We used the online version of the corpus available at: `https://ithub.korean.go.kr/user/corpus/corpusSearchManager.do`

[4]Ejels are tokens occurring between white spaces and they roughly correspond to words in English.

in such a way that the verb occurs with nouns indicating some kind of mood/atmosphere.

(14) a. phwungnyen-i tun tulnyek-ul
bumper-year-NOM enter field-ACC
talli-mye kaul-ul masy-ess-ta.
drive-while autumn-ACC drink-PST-DECL

'(lit.) While driving along the fields with a bumper year, I drank the autumn.' (Google, 2017, Newspaper)

b. cikum-kkaci pwunwiki-lul
now-until atmosphere-ACC
masy-ess-tamyen icey pwunwiki-ey
drink-PST-if now atmosphere-by
chwiha-y-po-ca.
be.intoxicated-CONN-try-SUG

'(lit.) So far we have drunk the atmosphere. Let's now get intoxicated by the atmosphere.' (Google, 2013, Newspaper)

In these metaphorical examples with *masi-* 'drink', the agent experiences the mood or atmosphere indicated/triggered by the object. Given that we can feel a certain mood/atmosphere by means of the air around the area, we can assume that these are further extended metaphorical instances of DRINKING IS INHALING.

3.4 Conceptual metaphorical extensions of *mek-* 'eat'

The Korean ingestive verb *mek-* 'eat' can have various types of conceptual metaphorical extensions. One conceptual metaphor whose examples are frequently observed in the Sejong corpus is EATING IS CONSUMING RESOURCES.

(15) a. hwaksilhi ani oto-ka
obviously well automatic.car-NOM
kilum-ul com mek-ki-n hay-twu,
fuel-ACC some eat-NMLZ-TOP do-but
pyenha-ki-n ha-nikka, ...
convenient-NMLZ-TOP do-because ...

'Well, obviously, automatic cars eat fuel somewhat but they are convenient, so ...' (Sejong corpus, 2001, Everyday conversation)

b. motun kacenceyphwum-un
all home.appliances-TOP
ceon-eyse koon-ulo
low.temperature-from high-temperature-to
ollaka-l-ttay kacang cenki-lul
go.up-FUT-when most electricity-ACC
manhi mek-nun-ta.
much eat-PRES-DECL

'All home appliances take most electricity when they go up to high temperature heat from low temperature heat.' (Sejong corpus, 1998, Magazine)

Similar to English, in these examples, an entity denoting some kind of resource such as fuel, electricity, and even expenses occurs along with the verb *mek-* 'eat', indicating that such a resource is consumed.

Another conceptual metaphor we can find from authentic corpus data is EATING IS ACQUIRING POSSESSION:

(16) a. tayhak kyoswu-tul-un pwuceng
college professor-PL-TOP illicit
iphak-ulo ton-ul mek-nun-ta.
admission-by money-ACC eat-PRES-DECL

"College professors take money by illicit admissions.' (Sejong corpus, 1991, Newspaper)

b. mikwuk-un philipin-ul mek-ko
America-TOP the.Philippines-ACC eat-and
ilpon-un hanpanto-lul
Japan-TOP the.Korean.Peninsula-ACC
mek-kyess-ta-ko ha-n kes-i
eat-FUT-DECL-COMP do-REL thing-NOM
kassula-tayphutu coyak-i-pnita.
Katsura-Taft treaty-be-DECL

'It is the Katsura-Taft agreement that states that the U.S. would acquire the Philippines and Japan the Korean Peninsula.' (Sejong corpus, 1990, Book)

In most cases involving this conceptual metaphor with *mek-* 'eat', acquiring possession is done in a rather illicit manner as shown in (16a) and (16b) similarly to its English counterpart with *eat*, although in some cases it is carried out rightfully.

In Korean, *mek-* 'eat' can also be metaphorically extended to the concept of suffering as in (17):

(17) a. etten acessi-eykey yok-ul
certain mister-by swear.word-ACC
mek-ess-ta.
eat-PST-DECL

'I got swear words from a middle-aged man.' (Sejong corpus, 1991, Book)

b. ku nyesek kemanhay. kolthang com
the punk arrogant trouble some
mek-ye-yaci.
eat-CAUS-want

'The punk is arrogant. I'd like to put him through trouble.' (Sejong corpus, 1985, Book)

c. kumnyen-ey-nun tewi-lul mek-ci
this.year-in-TOP heat-ACC eat-CONN
ma-la.
not-IMP

'Don't suffer heatstroke this year.' (Google, 1987, Book)

Metaphorical examples of this type contain verbal nouns like *yok* 'swear word', *cingpel* 'punishment', and common nouns like *kolthang/ay* 'trouble', *tewi* 'heat'. Some of them are concrete nouns such as *han pang* 'one punch' and *pheynelth kol* 'penalty goal', while others are rather abstract ones such as *tewi* 'heat' and *ay* 'trouble'.

Furthermore, the Korean ingestive verb *mek-* 'eat' can be metaphorically extended to winning/competing, inducing EATING IS WINNING/COMPETING as in (18):

(18) a. aye ephu mek-ul sayngkakha-n
at.all F eat-REL think-REL
ay-tul-un an nao-nikka, ...
child-PL-TOP not come-because,

'Those students who are thinking about getting an F do not come to this class at all, so ...' (Sejong corpus, 2003, Everyday conversation)

b. emma na il-tung mek-ess-e.
mom I first-place eat-PST-DECL

'Mom, I won the first place.' (Google, 2017, Newspaper)

Getting a good or bad grade involves competition and participating in an event which ranks participants based on a certain criterion also involves competition. Note that in cases like these the verb *mek-* 'eat' can co-occur with positive words like *il-tung* "first place" and *eyi* "A" and their negative counterparts like *kkol-tung* "last place" and *ephu* "F" as well.

Next, we also have the conceptual metaphor EATING IS HAVING THOUGHTS/FEELINGS:

(19) a. tantanhi mam-ul mek-ko cip-ul
firmly mind-ACC eat-and home-ACC
nase-ss-ta.
leave-PST-DECL

'I made up a firm mind and left home.' (Sejong corpus, 1991, Newspaper)

b. ce chwungkyek mek-e kacikwu
I shock eat-CONN because
kunyang nawa-ss-eyo.
just come.out-PST-DECL

'I was shocked, so I just came out.' (Sejong corpus, 2002, Topic conversation)

This conceptual metaphor seems to be derived from the internalization facet involved in the eating process.

We can often find metaphorical examples with *mek-* 'eat' that are related to lives in certain cultures or groups as well.

(20) a. nwukwu-n tayhak mwul an mek-e
who-TOP college water not eat-CONN
poa-ss-na?
see-PST-QUE

'Who hasn't been in college?' (Sejong corpus, 1993, Book)

b. koawenpap-ul han sipnyen
orphanage.rice-ACC about ten.years
mek-ess-ta.
eat-PST-DECL

'I lived in an orphanage for 10 years. (Sejong corpus, 1994, Book)

In most cases of this conceptual metaphor EATING IS LIVING DIFFERENT TYPES OF CULTURES/LIVES, the verb *mek-* 'eat' combines with complex nouns involving *mwul* 'water' and *pap* 'rice'.

One more conceptual metaphor with *mek-* 'eat' concerns EATING IS GAINING AGE.

(21) a. icey-n nai-lul nemwu manhi
now-TOP age-ACC too much
mek-ess-e.
eat-PST-DECL

'I am now too old. (Sejong corpus, 2002, Book)

b. yel sal mek-un cokhaay-ka enni
ten age eat-REL nephew-NOM older.sister
aph-ul kalomak-ass-ta.
front-ACC block-PST-DECL

'My nephew who is 10 years old got in my sister's way.' (Sejong corpus, 2001, Book)

Given the general assumption that we usually eat three meals a day, the more meals we eat, the older we are. In this regard, this conceptual metaphor EATING IS GAINING AGE has a bearing on the relationship between eating meals and gaining age.

The Korean verb *mek-* 'eat' also licenses a metaphorical extension to destroying:

(22) a. ely-ess-ul-ttay-nun Attoatto-ka
young-PST-REL-when-TOP Attoatto-NOM
ai-tul-ey tayhan kiek-man-ul
child-PL-to about memory-only-ACC
mek-nun-ta-ko
eat-PRES-DECL-COMP
sayngkakha-yess-supnita.
think-PST-DECL

'When I was young, I thought that Attoatto only ate children's memory.' (Sejong corpus, 2002, Book)

b. keyulum-i insayng-ul mek-e
laziness-NOM life-ACC eat-CONN
chiwu-n-ta.
throw.away-PRES-DECL

'Laziness eats away your life.' (Google, 2007, Blog)

Just like the English verb *eat*, its Korean counterpart *mek-* 'eat' can be metaphorically extended in such a way that the agent affects some type of destruction of the object.

Like the English ingestive verb *eat*, the Korean verb *mek-* 'eat' can be metaphorically extended to sexual activity, too:

(23) ku-nun pelsse yele yeca-lul
he-TOP already several woman-ACC
mek-ess-ta.
eat-PST-DECL

'He has already slept with several women.' (Google, 2016, Dictionary)

This is more of a slang expression but still is a type of conceptual metaphor with *mek-* 'eat' with high enough frequency.

Finally, with *mek-* 'eat', the conceptual metaphor EATING IS BEING EFFECTIVE is available:

(24) a. ilen nonli-ka elmana
this logic-NOM how
mek-hi-lci-nun uymwun-i-ta.
eat-PASS-QUE-TOP question-be-DECL

'The question is how effective this logic will be.' (Sejong corpus, 2003, Newspaper)

b. ta phokiha-yess-ten cakcen-i tutie
all give.up-PAST-PST strategy-NOM finally
mek-hi-n kes-i-ta.
eat-PASS-REL thing-be-DECL

'The strategy that we had almost given up was finally effective.' (Sejong corpus, 2002, Book)

This conceptual metaphor always involves the passive form of the verb *mek-* 'eat'.

4 Comparisons between English and Korean

In this section, we discuss similarities between metaphorical extensions of *eat* and *drink* in English and their Korean counterparts and their differences.

4.1 Main similarities

The two typologically different languages, English and Korean, exhibit similar behavior in diverse respects, in terms of conceptual metaphorical extensions with *eat* and *drink* verbs.

(25) DRINKING IS INHALING

a. We drink the air before us. (COCA, 1993, Academic)

b. malkun kongki-lul masi-myense, ...
fresh air-ACC drink-and, ...

'We drank fresh air and ...' (Sejong corpus, 2002, Book)

(26) DRINKING/EATING IS CONSUMING RESOURCES

a. His old car was eating up the gas. (COCA, 1996, Fiction)

b. hwaksilhi ani oto-ka
obviously well automatic.car-NOM
kilum-ul com mek-ki-n hay-twu,
fuel-ACC some eat-NMLZ-TOP do-but
pyenha-ki-n ha-nikka, ...
convenient-NMLZ-TOP do-because ...

'Well, obviously, automatic cars eat fuel somewhat but they are convenient, so ...' (Sejong corpus, 2001, Everyday conversation)

(27) EATING IS ACQUIRING POSSESSIONS

a. Asia is eating into corporate profits. (COCA, 1998, Spoken)

b. mikwuk-un philipin-ul mek-ko
America-TOP the.Philippines-ACC eat-and
ilpon-un hanpanto-lul
Japan-TOP the.Korean.Peninsula-ACC
mek-kyess-ta-ko ha-n kes-i
eat-FUT-DECL-COMP do-REL thing-NOM
kassula-tayphutu coyak-i-pnita.
Katsura-Taft treaty-be-DECL

'It is the Katsura-Taft agreement that states that the U.S. would acquire the Philippines and Japan the Korean Peninsula.' (Sejong corpus, 1990, Book)

(28) EATING IS DESTROYING

a. Jealousy eats away at the soul, you know, Benjamin. (COCA, 1990, Spoken)

b. keyulum-i insayng-ul mek-e
laziness-NOM life-ACC eat-CONN
chiwu-n-ta.
throw.away-PRES-DECL

'Laziness eats away your life.' (Google, 2007, Blog)

(29) EATING IS FULFILLING BASIC NATURAL DESIRES

a. Somebody else ate her pussy, sure. (COCA, 2010, Fiction)

b. ku-nun pelsse yele yeca-lul
he-TOP already several woman-ACC
mek-ess-ta.
eat-PST-DECL

'He has already slept with several women.' (Google, 2016, Dictionary)

As demonstrated in these examples, English and Korean use similar conceptual metaphors with 'eat' and 'drink' verbs in several different domains and this can be attributed to basic conceptual meaning components the two languages have in common for those ingestive verbs. Note, in addition, that all the conceptual metaphors with *eat* found in English are a subset of conceptual metaphors wth *mek-* 'eat' in Korean, meaning that the Korean verb *mek-* 'eat' has more diverse conceptual metaphorical extensions than the English verb *eat*.

4.2 Main differences

Although English and Korean show similar behavior in a variety of respects with respect to conceptual metaphorical extensions with *eat* and *drink* verbs, they also display differences in some respects. For instance, different conceptual metaphors are observed frequently and some are given in the following table:

Conceptual metaphor	Korean	English
DRINKING IS LISTENING	*umak-ul masita	drink music
EATING IS SUFFERING	yok-ul mek-ta	*eat swear words
EATING IS WINNING/COMPETING	il-tung mek-ta ephu-lul mek-ta	*eat the first place *eat an F
EATING IS HARBORING THOUGHTS/FEELINGS	maum-ul mek-ta chungkyek-ul mek-ta	*eat a mind *eat shock
EATING IS LIVING DIFFERENT TYPES OF CULTURE/LIVES	tayhakmwul-ul mek-ta koanwenpap-ul mek-ta	*eat college water *eat orphanage rice
EATING IS GAINING AGE	nai-lul mek-ta	*eat ages
EATING IS BEING EFFECTIVE	nonli-ka mek-hi-ta	*logic is eaten

Some of these differences come from cultural differences between Korea and U.S., while others are just idiosyncrasies in the two languages. For instance, historically speaking, in Korea eating had not been an easy thing to do for normal people until very recently (Song, 2009). This provides an explanation why we have the conceptual metaphor EATING IS SUFFERING in Korean and other conceptual metaphors with *mek-* 'eat' have negative semantic prosody, which is not observed in English. In addition, steamed rice is the most crucial part in the traditional Korean meal; thus, we have numerous examples with *pap* 'rice' in the EATING IS LIVING DIFFERENT CULTURES/LIVES. Furthermore, eating meals is a daily activity and the more meals we eat, the older we are. This conceptualization is realized in the metaphorical extension with *mek-* 'eat' in Korean, but it is not the case in English. On the other hand, the conceptual metaphor EATING IS BEING EFFECTIVE is idiosyncratic in the sense that it is available only in Korean with the passive marker on the verb *mek-* 'eat', but not in English.

5 Conclusion

This paper has examined conceptual metaphorical extensions with ingestive verbs in English and Korean with particular focus on 'eat' and 'drink' verbs on the basis of authentic corpus data. We have seen that both English and Korean employ varied metaphorical extensions of the two ingestive verbs. We have also observed that the two languages overlap in many different conceptual metaphorical extensions, but display some different conceptual metaphorical extensions as well. The differences may be caused by linguistic as well as cultural differences.

References

Hook, Peter and Prashant Pardeshi. 2009. The Semantic Evolution of EAT-expressions: Ways and Byways. In John Newman (ed.), *The Linguistics of Eating and Drinking*, 153-172. Amsterdam: John Benjamins Publishing Company.

Jeon, Mi Ae. 2016. Metaphorical and metonymical uses of the Korean verb *meok*. Master's thesis, University of Malaya.

Lee, Yang-Hye. 2002. Meokttauy Uymiwa Kineung Pyenhwa (Meaning and Function Change of 'Meoktta (Eat)'). *Korean Linguistics*, 15:185-210.

Lee, Yang-Hye. 2012. A Study on Teaching and Learning Method of Multi-Function and Meaning of Korean 'Meoktta (Eat)'. *Wulimalyenkwu*, 30:297-325.

Næss, Ashild. 2009. How Transitive are EAT and DRINK Verbs? In John Newman (ed.), *The Linguistics of Eating and Drinking*, 27-43. Amsterdam: John Benjamins Publishing Company.

Newman, John. 1997. Eating and Drinking as Sources of Metaphor in English. *Cuadernos de Filologia Inglesa*, 6(2):213-231.

Newman, John. 2009. A Cross-linguistic Overview of 'Eat' and 'Drink'. In John Newman (ed.), *The Linguistics of Eating and Drinking*, 1-26. Amsterdam: John Benjamins Publishing Company.

Song, Jae Jung. 2009. What (Not) to Eat or Drink : Metaphor and Metonymy of Eating and Drinking in Korean. In John Newman (ed.), *The Linguistics of Eating and Drinking*, 195-228. Amsterdam: John Benjamins Publishing Company.

Wierzbicka, Anna. 2009. All People Eat and Drink : Does This Mean that 'Eat' and 'Drink' are Universal Human Concepts? In John Newman (ed.), *The Linguistics of Eating and Drinking*, 65-90. Amsterdam: John Benjamins Publishing Company.

Yamaguchi, Toshiko. 2009. Literal and Figurative Uses of Japanese EAT and DRINK. In John Newman (ed.), *The Linguistics of Eating and Drinking*, 65-90. Amsterdam: John Benjamins Publishing Company.

Food-Related Sentiment Analysis for Cantonese

Natalia Klyueva[1], Yunfei Long[2], Chu-Ren Huang[1], Qin Lu[2],
[1]Department of Chinese and Bilingual Studies, The Hong Kong Polytechnic University
{natalia.klyueva,churen.huang}@polyu.edu.hk
[2]Department of Computing, The Hong Kong Polytechnic University
{csylong,csluqin}@comp.polyu.edu.hk

Abstract

In this paper, we describe a work in progress on collecting data from the domain of food reviews in Hong Kong for sentiment analysis and the initial experiments conducted on the data. Another goal of this study is to use the described data to create a sentiment lexicon for Cantonese, which will serve as a resource for opinion mining related machine learning experiments.

1 Introduction

Sentiment analysis is one of the most popular topics in Natural Language Processing, as the opinions of people present a very valuable asset for companies to develop and improve their products based on customer expectations and feedback. Luckily for this research area, product review comments and feedback are likely to be posted on the internet, free and in big quantity. User generated content is especially large in the domain of customer reviews, and that will be the source of our data - reviews in the food domain.

The approaches in automatic text classification according to their polarity traditionally involved supervised machine learning methods. Various linguistic characteristics (like positive or negative words, part-of-speech patterns that can characterize polarity) of the text that potentially contained opinion bits served as features for a classifier.

Nowadays, the most widely used technique to encode words, sentences and even texts – word embeddings – Latest development in deep learning has found its way into the sentiment analysis in which words are represented by a dense vector learnt from embedding models such as word2vec or Doc2Vec.

One of the "linguistic" knowledge that can potentially improve the accuracy of sentiment analysis are sentiment lexicons or more complex emotion lexicons. They are integrated into the machine learning pipeline, e.g. (S.K.Rastogi et al., 2014). Sentiment lexicons are important resources for sentiment analysis. These lexicons consist of predetermined list of words assigned to sentiment labels or values, which is baseline for many machine learning based methods(Liu and Zhang, 2012; Tabak and Evrim, 2016; Long et al., 2017). Depending on sentiment models, there are two mainstream labeling schemas. The first schema is representing affective meanings of words by discrete sentiment labels, such as as positive, negative, etc (Ekman et al., 1983). The second schema is to represent affective meanings by means of more comprehensive multi-dimensional representation models, like the valence-arousal dominance model (VAD) (Russell, 1980) and the evaluation-potency-activity model (EPA) (Heise, 1965).

Sentiment lexicons are heavily investigated in English (Gilbert, 2014; Li et al., 2017) and Chinese (Wang and Ku, 2016). However, building sentiment lexicon for low-resources languages or dialects is not an easy task. That is why we decided to collect and investigate the text in Cantonese. Cantonese is a variety of Chinese spoken in the city of Guangzhou (historically known as Canton) and its surrounding area in southeastern China, including HK SAR and Macao SAR [1]. Compared to the studies on Man-

[1]https://en.wikipedia.org/wiki/Cantonese

darin, studies on Cantonese are still in the infant stage and there is no available Cantonese sentiment lexicon useful for Cantonese sentiment analysis. In this paper, we present the initial attempts to build the lexicon with the help of students annotation.

This paper is structured as follows. First, in Section 2 we describe how we collected and processed the data from the web. In Section 3 we show the data pre-processing and implementation of a baseline classification models. In Section 4 we derive a sentiment lexicon that can be integrated into the machine learning pipeline to improve the baseline results. So far this experiment is yet to be completed. We conclude and show the plans for future in Section 5.

2 Data collection

The data were collected from the web site with reviews of food and restaurants in Hong Kong `www.openrice.com` using python scrapper (scrapy), with the permission of the portal owner to perform scientific (non-commercial) experiments with the data. The special restriction was made on user-sensitive data, like nickname and amount of money spent.

According the the customer reviews, the restaurants are assigned with a rank and the search can be done both according to the restaurant IDs and food name. The reviews are written mostly in Cantonese Chinese, but also in English and Mandarin Chinese. They feature exactly the information needed to perform sentiment analysis: text reviews and the scores that reflect customer opinion (sentiment). Figure 1 demonstrates the example of a review.

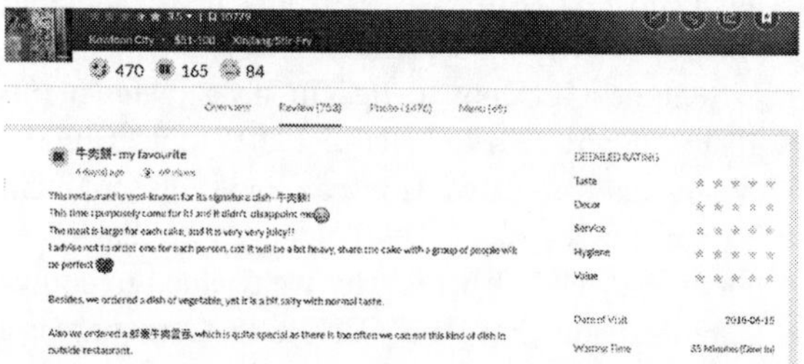

Figure 1: Example of a customer's review on openrice

During the crawling, the information from the web was extracted and stored into *json* format. The format of the crawled data is the following:

{"res_name": "清　　真　　牛　　肉 Islam Food", "res_id": "1441", "taste": 5, "environment": 3, "service": 3, "sanitation": 3, "worthy": 3, "title": "不能 的爆汁牛肉!!!", "comment": "九城. 不只是泰菜出名. 有不少地道特色的餐都非常有名. 人人都著朝....", "pictures": ...}

The statistics of the crawled data is presented in Table1

comments	360,701
restaurants	4,924
customers	about 60,000

Table 1: Crawled data: basic statistics

The raw data contained comments in 3 languages: Cantonese, Mandarin and English. Code-switching (e.g. mix of English and Cantonese) was observed in a number of cases. For our experiments we selected the comments that were mostly in Cantonese and could involve minor chunks/words in English.

3 Baseline Model for Sentiment Analysis

The standard approach to sentiment analysis in the domain of reviews generally includes the basic task - training the model to predict the sentiment score of a review. The first step includes text data encoding as vectors powered by Doc2Vec/Word2Vec models. [2] The output is a sentiment score/mark - which can be either binary (positive/negative) or on a larger scale including neutral.

In the initial stage of this experiment, we have selected only one type of label - the overall rating of the restaurant as displayed by the emoji in the interface.

We believe it to be the most representative evaluation tag of the review, the one that really reflects the *sentiment/opinion* of a customer.

In sentiment analysis, the classification can be performed either on a binary scale (positive vs. negative) or on a multi-class scale that is suggested by

[2] `https://github.com/RaRe-Technologies/gensim/blob/develop/docs/notebooks/doc2vec-lee.ipynb`

the data: rating from 1 to 5 stars. In our experiments we will compare both types. [3]

3.1 Data Preprocessing

In order to feed the data to the model, we needed to convert it to the format required by the framework. First, we filtered out the data points that do not contain reviews or are in a language other than Cantonese and created two sets: one for multi-class classification, another for binary classification, the statistics is presented in Table 2.

	multi-class	binary
whole data	360,000	n/a
cleaned data	26,549	4,450

Table 2: Summary of the corpus size, number of reviews for data with multi-class classification (review scores on slace 1-5), and for the data with binary (1 or 5 star score) classification

The second step was text tokenization. As the Doc2Vec input should present sentences segmented into words, we tokenized Chinese text using Jieba segmentor (`https://github.com/fxsjy/jieba`). The website did not specify any metrics to measure accuracy of the tool, so we just relied on it as the most popular tokenizer for Chinese.

3.1.1 Text Encoding: Doc2Vec

In our experiment – unlike in the original Doc2Vec tutorial – we used unlabeled documents-reviews (the reviews are not labeled). After preprocessing the reviews (cleaning, tokenization), we trained the model on the openrice data using Doc2Vec implementation. We choose the vector size of 100, so that each review is encoded into the array of this size. After training the model, we substituted the reviews in the corpus with the respective vector according to the model and thus the text data became numerical and could had served as input for standard classifiers.

The side-effect of the trained model is its capability to represent relations between words or sentences (Mikolov et al., 2013). We tested on the following cases just to demonstrate the power of word analogies as measured in the vector space:

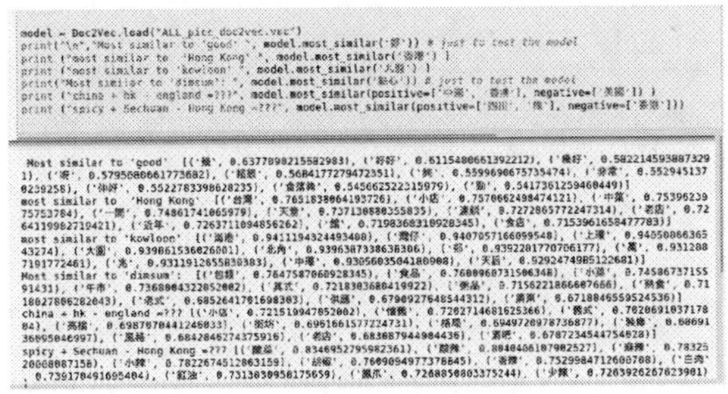

Figure 2: Lexical relations obtained from the model using the function *most_similar*

3.2 Preliminary Experiments

In our preliminary experiments, we trained three classifiers using *sklearn* python library:

- Logistic regression (logreg)
- Support Vector Machines (SVM)
- k-Nearest Neighbours

We conducted the following experiments; results are summarized in Table 3:

- **Multi-class classification**. For this, we used all the reviews that were ranked on the scale from 1 to 5 (in stars). The average accuracy for the classifiers was about 0.5.

  Such a low score can be attributed to the fact that the sentiment scale was quite large - from 1 to 5, and there is not much typical 'emotion' expression in the neutral (score 3) reviews.

- **binary classification** We took only the reviews with a either very negative (1) or very positive (5) score. For the same experiments setup the accuracy was much higher than for the baseline with all 5 sentiment classes.

Above all, we tested those setups for the whole data and for the half-size data to explore correlation between data size and accuracy of classifiers. It demonstrates that with bigger data the accuracy does not change at all for multi-scale classification

[3]The scripts with a small sample of data are available at: `https://github.com/polyu-llt/openrice_annotations`

	all-multi	all-bi	half-multi	half-bi
Logreg	0.493	0.854	0.477	0.773
SVM	0.464	0.854	0.469	0.775
Kneigh	0.408	0.823	0.408	0.77

Table 3: ML experiments: Logistic regression, SVM and k-neighbours; for all data, and half-size data

and only gets a little bit higher for a binary classifier.

As we have mentioned in the introduction, one of the possible ways to improve precision of the prediction is introducing the sentiment lexicon – a list of words that will help to identify polarity of the comment. In the next section, we describe work in progress on the deriving the lexicon.

4 Sentiment Lexicon via Crowd-sourcing

In order to get the polarity (evaluative) words to form the lexicon, we asked the students from the linguistic department to annotate the evaluative words alongside with the polarity and the aspect – a word to which the candidate word/phrase is related.

4.1 Setup of the Experiment

60 students were asked to annotate an excel file containing 20 comments. To measure the inter-annotator agreement, comments were randomly assigned twice to two different students. The evaluative labels from crawled data were not shown to the students.

4.2 Annotation Guidelines

For each evaluative word found in a comment students were requested to attach:

- the aspect word (the object/service/meal) that is being evaluated
- the sentiment (evaluative) word
- the sentiment mark ('+' - positive; '-' - negative; '0' - neutral).

They had to put the above information into one of five columns–categories to which evaluation relates: 'taste words', 'overall words', 'environment words', 'service words', 'sanitation words' and 'worthy words'. Some evaluations could be 'general', not referring to any aspect, in this case the annotation had to be done without an aspect word:

Review: *Amazing experience*!!!

Annotation: overall column: Amazing experience+

The aspect words/phrases and sentiment words/phrases should be separated by a colon in case more than one is present in a review:

review: *Love the bread and the soup! The birthday soufflé dessert is surprisingly yummy! The staff though was so unfriendly and mean!*

Annotation:

- Taste column: bread:love+; soup:love+; soufflé dessert: surprisingly yummy+
- Service column : staff:so unfriendly-/mean-

Different examples of sentiment words should be separated by semicolon (';'). If for one aspect there were more evaluative words, they were separated by a pipe: ('|'):

Example: good and yummy beef, but was too salted

Annotation: Taste column: beef:good+|yummy+|too salted-

Example in Cantonese('taste' column):

(1) 羊架: 最欣+
roast-sheep-neck: most-appreciated
'roast-sheep-neck: most-appreciated'

4.3 Lexicon Cleanup

We collect 600 comments from 60 native speaker students. We take the intersection of lexicon between two different annotators. The intersected words are then fed into second round of human checking. Together we get 1,887 positive words (Positive_words.txt) and 858 negative words(Negative_words.txt).

The resource with raw (unprocessed) annotations as well as the cleaned lexicon can be found at [4].

The sentiment lexicon was intended to serve as additional data for machine learning experiments

[4]https://github.com/polyu-llt/openrice_annotations/tree/master/annotations

that we will describe in Future work section. However, it will have a value on its own, as data for linguistic analysis for a low-resource language.

5 Conclusion and Future work

In this paper, we presented our research project on food-related sentiment analysis for Cantonese language. We described how the data were collected from the web openrice, showed the preliminary machine learning experiments on the data. For binary classification the results displayed higher accuracy than in the case of multi-class classification.

As for future work, we plan to integrate the sentiment lexicon for Cantonese into the ML pipeline. We also illustrated the steps for creating the lexicon by means of crowdsourcing, as well as the guidelines presented to the students for the annotation of positive and negative words in the reviews.

6 Acknowledgements

This work has been supported by the postdoctoral fellowship grant of the Hong Kong Polytechnic University (PolyU RTVU), project code G-YW2P; and GRF grant (CERG PolyU 15211/14E, PolyU 152006/16E).

References

Paul Ekman, Robert W Levenson, and Wallace V Friesen. 1983. Autonomic nervous system activity distinguishes among emotions. *Science*, 221(4616):1208–1210.

CJ Hutto Eric Gilbert. 2014. Vader: A parsimonious rule-based model for sentiment analysis of social media text. In *Eighth International Conference on Weblogs and Social Media (ICWSM-14). Available at (20/04/16) http://comp. social. gatech. edu/papers/icwsm14. vader. hutto. pdf.*

David R Heise. 1965. Semantic differential profiles for 1,000 most frequent english words. *Psychological Monographs: General and Applied*, 79(8):1.

Minglei Li, Qin Lu, Yunfei Long, and Lin Gui. 2017. Inferring affective meanings of words from word embedding. *IEEE Transactions on Affective Computing*, (1):1–1.

Bing Liu and Lei Zhang. 2012. A survey of opinion mining and sentiment analysis. In *Mining text data*, pages 415–463. Springer.

Yunfei Long, Lu Qin, Rong Xiang, Minglei Li, and Chu-Ren Huang. 2017. A cognition based attention model for sentiment analysis. In *Proceedings of the 2017 Conference on Empirical Methods in Natural Language Processing*, pages 462–471.

T Mikolov, W.-T Yih, and G Zweig. 2013. Linguistic regularities in continuous space word representations. pages 746–751, 01.

James A Russell. 1980. A circumplex model of affect. *Journal of personality and social psychology*, 39(6):1161.

S S.K.Rastogi, Rohit Singhal, and Anil Kumar. 2014. An improved sentiment classification using lexicon into svm. 95:37–42, 06.

Feride Savaroğlu Tabak and Vesile Evrim. 2016. Comparison of emotion lexicons. In *HONET-ICT, 2016*, pages 154–158. IEEE.

Shih-Ming Wang and Lun-Wei Ku. 2016. Antusd: A large chinese sentiment dictionary. In *LREC*.

A corpus-based study of *braised* dishes in Chinese-English menus

Lily Lim
School of Languages and Translation
Macao Polytechnic Institute
llim@ipm.edu.mo

Abstract

Few studies have been carried out in Macao for menu translation in the past. With Macao being listed as the City of Gastronomy in 2017, the Macao restaurants started to catch the world's attention, and online menus have turned to be an important tool for attracting tourists. With quality translation for menus of Michelin-starred restaurants and those in five-star hotels, this study investigates how particular words or terms have been translated as to build a regular word set for students' learning. This paper studies the expression of the cooking method "braise" in the menu translation, based on a sample of 3,606 items from 27 restaurants (local Michelin, 5-star and high-class restaurants) and overseas (Australia). The data reveals that there is a full set of Chinese verbs that correspond to *braised* in menu translation, varying according to the particular collocation of cooking method and food.

1 Introduction

With Macao being designated as UNESCO Creative City of Gastronomy in November 2017, the food industry turns out to be the highlight of the tourist sector, and catches the attention of tourists worldwide. The Macao government also dedicates various resources for promoting the image of local restaurants and local food culture. To the tourists overseas, the menu of a restaurant becomes an important tool to "deliver" them "message" on what local delicacies are available or what special dishes make the restaurant a "must-visit" spot. The translation of a bilingual or multilingual menu with quality is then particularly important to a restaurant on whether it can attract more customers.

It is therefore vital to study the translation methods useful for menus, while building a corpus for restaurant menus which not only enables us to study the collocation of the lexical items, but is also important to investigate any tendencies or norms for rendering particular dishes or cooking methods. Some commonly-used terms for cooking, like fried rice, steamed fish, and roasted pork, can easily be translated into "炒飯", "蒸魚" and "燒肉". But for word like "braise", there might be various ways for its translation depending on the cooking method and collocated food. Based on a self-built corpus that consists of dish names in both Chinese and English, this paper investigates what regular set of words tend to be used to translate "braise" in high ranking restaurants or hotels both in Macau and overseas.

2 Collection of dish names

This study focuses on the translation of menus of top quality, and collected the online menus of restaurants with Michelin star or those located in 5-star hotels or the prestigious ones. The menus in these restaurants tend to be carefully produced involving professional translators.

To carry out this study, online menus from a total of 27 restaurants have been collected, which consist of 24 local ones and 3 from Australia. Of the local restaurants, 13 are Michelin starred ones. Of all collected menus, 20 menus are translated from Chinese to English and the rest are from English to Chinese. The total dish names amount to 3,606, with 2,330 entries from menus of Chinese to English translation, 981 entries from menus of English to Chinese translation, while 295 entries are from restaurants in Australia.

32nd Pacific Asia Conference on Language, Information and Computation
The 25th Joint Workshop on Linguistics and Language Processing
Hong Kong, 1-3 December 2018

3 Data analysis and results

The data analysis will be both quantitative and qualitative. The concordancing software HyConc is used for data analysis, as to facilitate the statistics of the needed information. As pointed by Leech (1992) that the most simple and popular tool for carrying out a computational-basis research is through the use of indexing program (p. 114), and HyConc V3.9.6 is a reliable and an ideal concordancing software that works with Chinese and English texts. HyConc incorporates three functions: (1) processing for monolingual corpus analysis, (2) processing for parallel corpus analysis and (3) pre-processing for corpus. It has been widely used, because it supports Unicode which allows Chinese characters to be transferred freely on different platforms (Liu, 2013). Unlike some other concordance software that have problems with displaying Chinese characters, Hyconc is rather reliable in this respect. With the function of parallel corpora analysis built in HyConc, the analysis can be conducted not only on the frequency of a particular lexis but also the translation between the source and target texts.

Our analysis process begins with the searching of word "braise" in both the STs and TTs (Figure 1), returning a total of 240 dish names with "braise" used in target English.

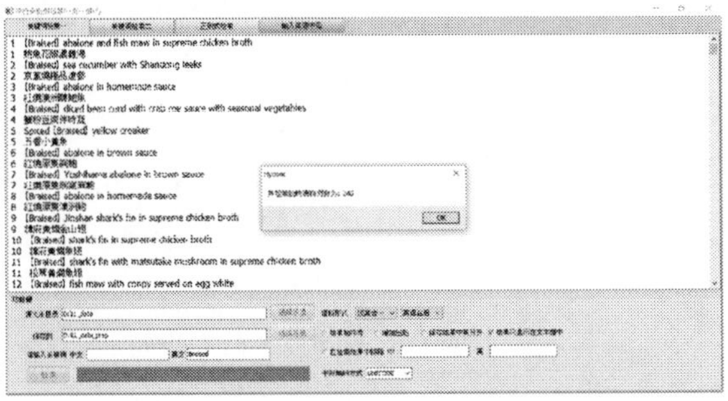

Figure 1: Searching for "braised" in HyConc

By examining this data, we further discovered nine Chinese verb types that correspond to "braise"– i.e., 燒 (shāo), 燜 (mèn)，扒 (pā)，炆 (wén)，撈 (lāo)，燴 (huì)，拆 (chāi), 煨 (wēi), and 扣 (kòu) (See Table 1). In fact, a significant number of Chinese dish names (n= 113) do not contain any verbs in Chinese but are translated into English with "braise", accounting for 47% of the 245 instances of "braised" dishes. For example, the Chinese dish named 蒜子火腩豆腐煲 is translated into *Braised Bean Curd with Garlic & Roast Pork Ribs*, in which 煲 bāo 'clay pot' entails the meaning of stewing food in clay pot, resulting in the use of "braise" in the English dish name. In addition, the most frequently used verb turned out to be 燒 shāo (n=56), which appears either by itself (n= 12) or in three collocations – i.e., 紅燒 hóng shāo 'braised in soy sauce' (n= 29), 蔥燒 cōng shāo 'braised with scallion' (n= 8) and 乾燒 gān shāo 'dry braised' (n= 7). The verb 燒 shāo and its collocations in Chinese therefore present the predominant type of verb phrase for "braised" dishes in our sample. There is also dialectal use of 炆 wén 'simmering' (n=5), which gives local Cantonese-speaking flavor.

Types of verbs	n=
no Chinese verb	113
燒	56
- 紅燒	29
- 蔥燒	8
- 乾燒	7
扣	20
扒	14
燴	13
燜	11
炆	5
撈	5
煨	2
拆	1
Total	240

Table 2: Verb Types in Chinese corresponding to "braised" in English

Our data shows that 47% (113 items) of the translation with the word "braise" is from Chinese dish names without occurrence of verb. Some of the examples are extracted below:

千層雙冬豆腐
Braised Bean Curd with Mushroom and Bamboo Shoot

順德花雕雞
Braised Chicken in Chinese Yellow Wine "Shunde Style"
蟹粉豆腐伴時蔬

Braised diced bean curd with crab roe sauce with seasonal vegetables
酸辣蹄筋
Braised pig tendon with Yunnan ham, sliced bamboo shoot and wild mushroom
麻婆豆腐
Braised bean curd with minced beef, Sichuan peppercorn and broad bean paste
饞嘴牛蛙
Braised bullfrog with angled luffa, spring onion pickled ginger and chili
壇子肉
Braised pork knuckle with chicken, thousand year egg and dried bamboo shoot

In the above examples, the source names of dishes in Chinese do not contain any Chinese verb about cooking. However, the word *braised* is used in the translation, and there is a regular pattern of *braised* collocating with bean curd and meat (chicken, pig tendon and bullfrog, etc.), while the prepositions "with" and "in" are used to expound the method of cooking. Instead of using literal translation, a very communicative translation is adopted with the addition of a great deal of details on ingredients and explicitation of cooking method in order to convey a more comprehensive idea to the foreign customers on how the dishes look like or taste like. The notably long English dish names are also the feature as described by Jurafsky (2014) that the use of longer words to describe a dish is a feature pertaining to expensive restaurants. Our study lends support to Jurafsky's observation, because the most lengthy dish names in our sample were collected from a restaurant of five-star hotel.

Apart from the "braised" dishes that do not contain Chinese verbs, the dishes with Chinese verbs on the cooking method (53% of our sample) reveal the types of food that tend to collocate with these verbs:

燒 (vegetable, toufu, duck, pork, lamb brisket and seafood);
紅燒 (mainly with shark's fin and abalone, followed by fish maw, tofu, pork belly, fish fillet, yam and beef brisket);
蔥燒 (all with sea cucumber except one with pig tendon and one with garoupa fillet);
焖 (mainly with seafood, and also with tofu and Chinese egg plant)
扒 (all with vegetable except one with fish maw and one with bird's nest)
燴 (mainly with shark's fin, followed by bird's nest, and a few instances of pork, sea cucumber and bean curd sheet)
乾燒 (seafood and E-Fu noodle)
炆 (abalone, fin, beef ribs, E-Fu noodle, and pomelo skin)
撈 (exclusively for shark's fins)
煨 (sea cucumber and shark's fin)
拆 (with crab meat)
扣 (mainly with goose web, followed pork belly, abalone, fish maw and sea cucumber)

The meats and vegetables that collocate with various types of Chinese verb for "braise" are presented in Table 2, with the information on frequency count and percentage.

Types of verbs	n=	Meat		Vegetable	
紅燒	29	fish maw beef brisket sea cucumber bird nest pork belly fish fillet abalone Shark fin	3.4% 3.4% 6.9% 6.9% 6.9% 6.9% 17% 37.9%	Yam bean curd	3.4% 6.9%
蔥燒	8	pig tendon pork belly garoupa fillet fish maw sea cucumber	12.5% 12.5% 12.5% 12.5% 62.5%	ginger scallion spring onion leek	25% 25% 25% 37.5%
乾燒	7	shark fin abalone lobster ball pork fish	14.28% 14.28% 14.28% 28.57% 28.57%	bean curd mushroom bean sprout celery	14.28% 14.28% 28.57% 28.57%
扣	20	shrimp roe salt fish abalone pork sea cucumber fish maw goose web	5% 5% 15% 25% 30% 30% 35%	mushroom eggplant preserved vegetable	5% 5% 15%

(Table 2 continued)

Types of verbs	n=	Meat		Vegetable	
扒	14	scallop crab claw fish seafood	7% 7% 7% 7%	winter melon bean sprout bean curd onion	7% 7% 7% 7%

		duck	7%	choy sum	7%
		beef	7%	potato	7%
		lamb	7%	bamboo piths	21%
		chicken	14%	pineapple	21%
		beef	14%	mushroom	28.5%
		pork chop	14%	seasonal	
		bird nest	21%	vegetable	42.85%
		prawn	28.5%		
		ham	42.8%		
		crab meat	42.8%		
燴	13	Lobster	7.69%	bean curd	7.69%
		conpoy	7.69%	lily bulb	7.69%
		fish	7.69%	bay leaves	7.69%
		pork	7.69%	preserved	7.69%
		gizzard	7.69%	vegetables	7.69%
		birdnest	7.69%	Mushroom	15.3%
		Abalone	7.69%		
		Octopus	7.69%		
		Bacon	7.69%		
		Ox tongue	7.69%		
		Seafood	15.3%		
		Shrimp	15.3%		
		Sea cucumber	23%		
扒	14	scallop	7%	winter melon	7%
		crab claw	7%	bean sprout	7%
		fish	7%	bean curd	7%
		seafood	7%	onion	7%
		duck	7%	choy sum	7%
		beef	7%	potato	7%
		lamb	7%	bamboo piths	21%
		chicken	14%	pineapple	21%
		beef	14%	mushroom	28.5%
		pork chop	14%	seasonal	
		bird nest	21%	vegetable	42.85%
		prawn	28.5%		
		ham	42.8%		
		crab meat	42.8%		
燴	13	Lobster	7.69%	bean curd	7.69%
		conpoy	7.69%	lily bulb	7.69%
		fish	7.69%	bay leaves	7.69%
		pork	7.69%	preserved	7.69%
		gizzard	7.69%	vegetables	7.69%
		birdnest	7.69%	Mushroom	15.3%
		Abalone	7.69%		
		Octopus	7.69%		
		Bacon	7.69%		
		Ox tongue	7.69%		
		Seafood	15.3%		
		Shrimp	15.3%		
		Sea cucumber	23%		

Table 2: Distribution of the collocation of meats and vegetables with each type of verb

According to Merriam-Webster English dictionary, the definition of *braise* means to have food cooked slowly in a closed pot, and the Chinese term *炆* is used in Lu Gusun's *The English-Chinese Dictionary* (2007). Our data shows that a variety of Chinese verbs for cooking are related to *braise* in English. Depending on the way of cooking and the collocation of food, translators can use corresponding Chinese verbs in addition to *炆* for the appropriate expression.

Comparing to the collected data from Chinese menus, the English menus have much fewer dishes with the names containing *braise*. From a total of 981 dish names, there are only two dishes, which account for only 0.2% of the total dishes. The two dishes are *Octopus Braised in Olive Oil with Garlic, Peppers and Sautéed Spinach Corn Bread (欖油燜八爪魚配香蒜，波椒及薯仔)* and *Braised Grouper Fillet with Thyme and Buttered Clam Sauce (石斑魚柳配蜆汁)*. While the Chinese menus (which are first written in Chinese) have roughly 10% (240 out of 2330) of dishes translated as *braised* dishes, the English menus (which are first written in English) have around 50 times less. This can be due to the reason that the Chinese menus were collected from the Chinese restaurants, whereas the English menus were mainly collected from Portuguese restaurants, and also some French, Italian and Indian restaurants. The figures strongly suggest that cooking food with slow fire in a closed pot is typical for Chinese cuisine.

The menus collected from the Chinese restaurants in Australian revealed similar findings. – There are 25 braised dishes in a total of 295 dishes, accounting for around 8.5% of the total, which is close to our finding of 10% in the local menus in Macau. The dish names collected from Australian presented similar expressions in Chinese and in the foods that collocate with *braised*, as shown below.

Without the use of Chinese verbs for cooking (16 items)

扒 (6 items) with duck and vegetable

紅燒 (2 items) with fish fillet and tofu

焗 (1 item) with pork ribs

Similar to the previous findings on the local menus of Chinese restaurants, the data from overseas menus again show that the Chinese dish names without verbs account for 64% (16/25) of the total dishes. However, the data of the local menus does not have 焗 *jú* 'baked' as a verb type for dishes with *braised* in their English names. The Chinese verb "焗" in the last example above is from the dish named "OK 汁焗肉排" with English translation *Braised pork ribs in OK sauce.* We can make reference to the local menus of the Chinese restaurants, in which there are two dishes of pork ribs, namely 蒜香肉排 (Salt & Pepper Spare Ribs with a Touch of Garlic) and 椒鹽肉排 (Deep-fried Pork Ribs with Peppercorn Salt). There is no verb "焗" in both Chinese names, while its commonly used English equivanlent is *baked.* This is evidenced by the data collected from the Portuguese restaurants, for examples, *Baked codfish with creamy sauce* (白汁焗馬介休), *Baked coconut chicken in Portuguese style* (焗葡國雞) and *Baked duck rice with cheese and Portuguese sausage* (芝士葡國腸焗鴨飯).

The instance of using "焗" for *braised* dish name in English can be a result of a mixed cuisine culture, as the Chinese restaurant that uses this dish name is located in Australia. Baking food is a typical western style and favorite dishes for Australians. By including the verb "焗" in the Chinese name of the dish can be an attraction to the Australian Chinese, and a reflection of a western style with OK sauce, which is a brand of brown sauce originated from the UK. The use of the word *braised,* on the other hand, is a reflection of Chinese style of cooking, which may sound exotically interesting to Australian clients.

Types of verbs	This sample	CCL	Sinica
燒	56 (49%)		
- 紅燒	29 (25%)	555 (19%)	25 (42%)
- 蔥燒	8 (7%)	27 (1%)	3 (5%)
- 乾燒	7 (6%)	63 (2%)	0 (0%)
扣	20 (17%)	72 (2%)	0 (0%)
扒	14 (12%)	125 (4%)	0 (0%)
燴	13 (11%)	563 (19%)	7 (12%)
燜	11 (10%)	873 (30%)	13 (22%)
炆	5 (4%)	76 (3%)	2 (3%)
撈	5 (4%)	2 (0%)	0 (0%)
煨	2 (2%)	577 (20%)	9 (15%)
拆	1 (1%)	10 (0%)	0 (0%)
Total	240 (100%)	2943 (100%)	59 (100%)

Table 3: Comparing the frequency of occurrence of the verbs: this sample, CCL and Sinica

Apart from our analysis of the samples collected from local restaurants, we also examined the verbs listed in Table 1 in large balanced corpora, looking at their occurrence in cooking situations in general. The aim is to reveal if the "braised" dishes in our sample entail a special distribution of meaning. Table 3 presents a comparison of the verbs in terms of occurrence count and percentage between this sample and two very representative balanced corpora of Modern Chinese – i.e., CCL and Sinica.

The comparison shows that the braised dishes in our sample entail a notably higher rate of occurrence of 紅燒, 蔥燒, 乾燒, 扣, 扒, 炆, 撈 and 拆, in particular 紅燒, 扣 and 扒. By contrast, 燴, 燜 and 煨 appear to be weakly associated with braised foods in our sample, although they are commonly used verbs for cooking in Chinese (see Table 3).

4 Conclusion

The data collected from three different sources for this study, including local Chinese, non-Chinese (mainly Portuguese restaurants) and overseas restaurants (Australia), has led to interesting findings that the term *braise* reflects typical Chinese cooking style, and has been widely used in the menu of Chinese restaurants to denote a variety of Chinese cooking methods, collocating with a wide range of seafood, vegetable and meat. This study has identified a set of Chinese verbs for cooking with fine-grained differences, although they can be expressed by the term *braise* as a general cover term. The set of Chinese verbs provides student translators with a wider range of word choice in addition to the few ones given by the dictionary. They will also have a better idea of when to have *braise* translated as rarely known verbs like 扒 *pā* , 撈 *lāo* or 拆 *chāi*, according to the cooking method and collocation of food and ingredients. This study points to the value of using corpus tools for vocabulary preparation (Lim 2014). It reveals, in particular, the usefulness of self-built specialised corpus, which enables translators or interpreters to conduct in-depth study on word choices for rendering food-related texts and to work out the contexts in which different choices fit. The findings inspire new methods for translator and interpreter training, in relation to their self-initiated use of IT tools (cf. Lim 2013; Wang and Lim 2017).

Even though the data from overseas is of a modest size, with around 300 items from three reputable Chinese restaurants in Australia, the research can be taken as a pilot study, which has resulted in useful findings that similarities in menu translation do exist between Macao and Australia, and that overseas menus tend to adapt to the western culinary culture in order to be more attractive to the local customers.

References

CCL (Center for Chinese Linguistics PKU). Retrieved from http://ccl.pku.edu.cn:8080/ccl_corpus/index.jsp

Dan Jurafsky. 2014. The Language of Food – A Linguist Reads the Menu. W. W. Norton & Company, New York.

Geoffrey N. Leech. 1992. Corpora and theories of linguistic performance. In Jan Svartvik (Ed.), Directions in Corpus Linguistics. Proceedings of Nobel Symposium 82, Stockholm, 4-8 August. Berlin/ New York: Mouton de Gruyter, 105-122.

Lily, Lim (2013) Examining students' perceptions of computer-assisted interpreter training. The Interpreter and Translator Trainer 7(1): 71-89.

Lily, Lim (2014) Engaging student interpreters in vocabulary building: Web search with computer workbench. ReCALL 26(3): 355 - 73.

Keqiang, Liu 劉克強 2013 語料庫檢索及處理分析軟體 HyConc 功能與特點. 蘭州交通大學學報 32(5): 頁 93-95.

Gusun, Lu 陸谷孫（主編）2007 英漢大詞典 (The English-Chinese Dictionary)（第二版）上海：上海譯文出版社

Sinica (Academia Sinica Balanced Corpus of Modern Chinese). Retrieved from http://asbc.iis.sinica.edu.tw/

Vincent X., Wang and Lily Lim (2017) How do translators use web resources? Evidence from the performance of English-Chinese translators. In Dorothy Kelly (ed.) Human Issues in Translation Technology. London: Routledge, pp. 63-79.

Pleasing to the Mouth or Pleasant Personality:
A corpus-based study of conceptualization of desserts in online Chinese food reviews

Yin Zhong
Faculty of Humanities,
The Hong Kong Polytechnic University
beth.zhong@connect.polyu.hk

Chu-Ren Huang
Department of Chinese & Bilingual Studies,
The Hong Kong Polytechnic University
churen.huang@polyu.edu.hk

Abstract

Description of flavours of desserts often involves a rich range of vocabulary. This paper investigates the real-life language describing tastes of desserts in Mandarin Chinese, extracting data from *Dazhong Dianping*, the most popular restaurant review website in China. Using the *Sketch Engine* as the primary tool to extract collocations, we found that 'mouthfeel' and 'personality', instead of direct descriptions of TASTE or SMELL, are the most dominant expressions. In particular, more than one hundred 'mouthfeel' words are identified, with strong tendency of positive polarity. The majority of 'mouthfeel' terms are tactile (sense of touch) in nature, which shall be considered as synaesthetic metaphors to depict TASTE. Moreover, these 'mouthfeel' words often collocate with words connoting pleasant personality, especially in terms of warm social interactions. In summary, due to its intensional rather than physical telicity, description of desserts shows significant cultural variations. On the one hand, the preferred words still retain the same telic purpose, i.e., to please the mouth; on the other hand, instead of using expressions conveying intensional bodily pleasure (sensuality/sexuality), Chinese focus both on the parochial bodily experience (pleasing the mouth) as well as the social-interactional (pleasant personality) to describe desserts.

1 Introduction

Bite into a Snicker (a chocolate bar), how do you describe its feeling in your mouth? Mmmm, thick and gooey with the caramel syrup, crunchy peanuts, with the chocolate melting in your oral cavity, sweet, creamy, smooth and slightly bitter chocolate richness, with the aroma wafting up into your nasal cavity. When it is all consumed, you are surely pleased and satisfied. Tasting is a complicated process which could not be separated from gustatory (taste), olfactory (smell), and tactile (touch) senses. Vision and hearing are also involved in a way, and on top of that, emotions. Researchers named this multisensory experience 'flavour perception' and studied it mainly from neurophysiological and psychological perspectives (see, e.g. Small, 2012; Spence, 2017). Although Chinese people probably believe that they are most knowledgeable when it comes to tasting food and drinks, as exemplified by a famous Chinese saying 「民以食為天」 (Food is Heaven), few attempts have been made to investigate the relationship between the multisensory flavour perception and their language used to describe this experience. This paper will focus on discussing how Chinese people talk about their feelings when they taste desserts which are not part of Chinese food culture. It attempts to add to the existing literature on the interrelationship among different sensory modalities and shed more light on the relationship between language, perception and cognition.

1.1 The meaning of 味 *wèi* 'taste'

When we try to identify descriptions for desserts in Chinese, we start with this question: 這個甜品的味道如何? (*Zhège tiánpǐn de wèidao rúhé?* 'How is the taste of this dessert?') Therefore, before we go further, the first concept that calls for clarification is the meaning of 味 / 味道 (*wèi/wèidao*) in Mandarin Chinese.

The original meaning of 味 *wèi* is elaborated as 滋味 *zīwèi* in *ShuoWenJieZi* in *Handian*[1], and the following sentence extracted from *Lüshi Chunqiu*[2]

[1] Accessed at http://www.zdic.net/

[2] Also known as "The [Spring and Autumn] Annals of Lü Buwei". It is an encyclopaedic Chinese classic text and a

best explains what 滋味 *zīwèi* means to Chinese people: 「若人之於滋味，無不說甘脆，而甘脆未必受也。」("It is like the case of the human attraction for rich flavours. Everyone likes what is sweet and crisp, but that does not mean that they will accept what is sweet and crisp when it is offered to them." Translated by Knoblck & Riegel (2000, p.329)). *Sweet* is what human beings could sense through the taste receptor cells found in the taste buds on the tongue, whereas there is no such taste receptor to account for *crisp* - it is more like a feeling in our oral cavity when we bite and chew. This suggests that the original meaning of 味 *wèi* contains both the gustation and tactile sensation, at least in Classical Chinese.

In the 6th edition of *Xiandai Hanyu Cidian (The Contemporary Chinese Dictionary)*, 味 *wèi* is literally defined as "the gustatory sensation produced in the tongue by contact with a substance" and "the olfactory sensation produced in the nose by contact with a substance", indicating its inseparability with gustatory and olfactory senses while having nothing to do with the tactile sense. However, when searching 味道 *wèidao* (the substitute for 味 *wèi* due to the development of disyllabic words in Modern Chinese) in the *Chinese Web 2011* (Mainland, simplified)[3] in the *Sketch Engine* (Kilgarriff *et al.,* 2004), it is found that this word could also coexist with words which may not strictly relate to gustatory or olfactory sense but is involved with the vocabulary from other sensory modalities, such as 鮮嫩 (*xiānnèn*, 'fresh and tender'), 辛辣 (*xīnlà*, 'pungent or spicy'), 爽口 (*shuǎngkǒu*, 'tasty and refreshing'), 清新 (*qīngxīn*, 'refreshing'), etc. It shows that even with a clear definition of 味 *wèi* or 味道 *wèidao* in the dictionary, this term is still a rather ambiguous concept for the Chinese. In fact, 味 *wèi* was instantiated as an 'umbrella term' which goes beyond gustatory sensation and collocates with all the sensory words in Chinese Buddhist texts (Xiong & Huang, 2016).

The fuzzy meaning of 味 *wèi* or 味道 *wèidao* in Chinese is tantamount to the loose and interchangeable use of *taste* and *flavour* in English.

compendium of philosophical works compiled under the Qin Dynasty.

[3] Accessed at https://the.sketchengine.co.uk/auth/corpora/

Scientifically and strictly speaking, *taste* literally refers to the recognition of substances by the taste buds, which relates to gustatory sensation only; while *flavour* is multimodal and engages a combination of all five senses (e.g. Mouritsen & Styrbæk, 2017; Spencer, 2016), and is especially influenced by "tactile, thermal, painful and/or kinaesthetic effects" (Klosse, 2014, p.22; Spence, 2016, p.374). Given the only word 味 *wèi* or 味道 *wèidao* in Chinese accounts for both *taste* and *flavour*, it further suggests that linguistically speaking, 味 *wèi* or 味道 *wèidao* is not limited to gustatory sensory only; other sensory descriptors which are deemed 'synaesthetic metaphors'[4] may also contribute to the understanding of tastes and flavours.

1.2 The meaning of 'dessert'

'Dessert' is originally a French word meaning "to de-serve, to remove what has been served" and was later developed by the British and then American in the eighteenth century to limit 'dessert' to sweet things only (Jurafsky, 2014, pp.171-176), like puddings, cake, ice cream, etc. By saying 'dessert', one does not refer to all sweet foods. For example, Chinese cuisine also consists of a variety of sweet items, like 糕點 (*gāodiǎn*, 'cakes and pastries') and Cantonese Tong Sui (literally translated as 'sugar water'), but 'dessert' in the current context refers to only western dessert which is served as the last course in a Western meal. It does not exist in "the grammar of cuisine" on a Chinese dining table (Jurafsky, 2014, p.177). Although western dessert is neither an integral part of a traditional Chinese meal nor an element of Chinese food culture, statistics collected from big data show that the younger generation in China has acquired a growing interest in dessert - among all types of restaurants in China, cake and bakery shops rank at the top (25%) among the generation born after 1990 ("Generation after 90s is not fond of Chinese cuisine any more", 2018[5]). Given the

[4] 'Synaesthetic metaphor' refers to the conception in one sensory modality could be modified by the conception from other sensory domains (see, e.g. Ullmann, 1957; Williams, 1976). For example, *sharp* [TOUCH/SOURCE] *taste* [TASTE/TARGET] - 'sharp' is a synaesthetic metaphor to modify TASTE, and the synaesthetic directionality is from TOUCH to TASTE.

[5] Accessed at http://k.sina.com.cn/article_6440155365_17fdef8e500100321r.html

craving for western desserts in contemporary China, one wonders how Chinese people describe things like desserts which are not originally part of their culture.

2 Previous Related Works and Research Questions

Firstly, linguistically speaking, taste descriptors are often derivatives from source nouns, referring to components and are ambiguous and polysemous in English (Ankerstein & Pereira, 2013, p.313). Winter (2016a, p.57) also confirms the denominal nature of gustatory vocabulary by claiming that 70% of the gustatory adjectives found in the dictionary are denominal with only 30% having verbal or adjectival origins, among which mostly are derived from food items, e.g. *buttery, cheesy, chocolatey, creamy, eggy, fruity, juicy, lemony, meaty, salty*. While taste sense was found to be particularly "nouny" in English (Strik Lievers & Winter, 2018), in Chinese, the vocabulary labelled as gustatory sensory in Zhao, Huang and Yun (2018) is all adjectives, such as 甘 (*gān*, 'sweet'), 甜 (*tián*, 'sweet'), 鹹 (*xián*, 'salty'), 鮮 (*xiān*, 'tasty'), 淡 (*dàn*, 'of mild taste'), 濃 (*nóng*, 'of intense taste'). This linguistic feature in Chinese is similar to linguistic descriptors describing food in Japanese and Korean. Strauss (2005, p.1444) claimed that an adjective derived from a noun like 'cream' would simply indicate the item is literally made from or contains cream or looks like 'cream' in Japanese and Korean.

Secondly, Backhouse (1994, p.13) called taste "a cultural sense", suggesting taste perception has a close relationship with society and is greatly embedded in the culture. In Chinese, Wu (1989) found that the word 辣 (*là*, 'pungent') only exists in those regions where people are fond of eating spicy food because of the climate and environment. Besides that, there are only words for bitter, pungent and sour in Uyghur. Moreover, in Maqiao, a village in Jiangsu Province, all tasty things are described with just one word 甜 (*tián*, 'sweet') and all the desserts are called 糖 (*táng*, 'sweets') (Han, 1996). Apart from these manifestations from different linguistic concepts in various cultures, tastes are also associated with the diverse notions in different cultures. Strauss (2005) asserted that the emphasis on "softness, creaminess or sweetness" in American food commercials suggest sensual hedonism and pleasure in Western culture whereas in Japanese, the lack of vocabulary capturing the notion of "creaminess or richness" coupled with a focus on "lightness and airiness" reflect "a sense of purity and innocence" in Eastern culture. The hedonistic feature of food is likewise manifested in Jurafsky (2014)'s discussion of the association between sex and dessert. In the million online food reviews, Jurafsky (2014) identified most commonly used words to describe dessert are those from tactile sensation for describing textures and temperatures, such as "rich, moist, sticky, gooey, smooth, spongy, melting". These expressions are claimed to imply veiled sexual connotations and focus strongly on the feeling in the mouth, rather than the "appearance, smell, taste, or sound" (Jurafsky, 2014, p.103).

Last but not least, taste is also said to involve evaluation, pleasant or unpleasant, like 甜 (*tián*, 'sweet') to denote a pleasant feeling while 苦 (*kŭ*, 'bitter') to describe the opposite. With a focus on gustatory and olfactory lexicon, Winter (2016b) proposed that these two domains are associated with "more affective and emotional loaded content" with gustatory words being more positive and tend to occur in more positive contexts than olfactory items. Other relevant evaluative features of taste items are seen in Jurafsky (2014)'s mentioning of dessert reviews. He claimed that people have overwhelmingly positive sentiment for dessert, frequently using positive words like "delicious, yummy, fabulous, awesome" when discussing desserts (Jurafsky, 2014, p.104). It is apparent that, in general, positive words occur much more often than negative words in online food reviews. Jurafsky (2014) attributed this phenomenon to the "Pollyanna effect" (also known as "Pollyanna principle" or "positivity bias"), meaning people tend to remember pleasant items more accurately than unpleasant ones.

Since no comparable study has been conducted previously to investigate how Chinese people use sensory vocabulary to narrate their taste experience in real life, this study takes the initiative to build a DESSERT corpus containing online restaurant reviews from the largest restaurant review website *Dazhong Dianping*[6] (also known as 'Dianping' or

[6] It was established in 2003 and acts as a leading online city life guide and one of the first online consumer service rating

'Meituan-Dianping[7]') in Mainland China so as to examine current expressions used in Chinese to describe taste and flavour of desserts. In particular, this paper will address the following three research questions:

a. What words are frequently used to describe taste and flavour of desserts in Mandarin Chinese and what are the linguistic characteristics of these words?
b. How sensory vocabulary and sensory modalities interrelate, i.e., what kind of synaesthetic metaphors are used when describing tastes and flavours of desserts in Mandarin Chinese?
c. How desserts are represented and conceptualized in Chinese culture through the vocabulary used to describe desserts in Mandarin Chinese?

3 Data and Methodology

The DESSERT corpus consists of a total of over 4 million tokens in Simplified Chinese. The data was culled from the online reviews on 30 bakeries and cafés in Beijing, Shanghai and Guangzhou on the website of *Dazhong Dianping*. The shops are listed in a descending order according to the total number of reviews, thus, the 30 shops are those with the most number of comments in the three cities. But not all shops receiving the most comments were chosen as some shops are of the same type. Therefore, for example, only one branch of *Starbucks* is selected. Among the 30 shops, 10 of them are in Beijing, 10 in Shanghai and the other 10 in Guangzhou. This is because firstly, the three cities are among the top first-tier cities in China, the numbers of restaurants and netizens in *Dazhong Dianping* shall constitute a considerable proportion; secondly, it is considered that the distribution across northern, central and southern parts of China will help to reduce the influence of dialects spoken in any particular region. Lastly, those chosen restaurants were further checked to make sure most of the foods sold there are western desserts. As for comments, only comments under the categories of "Positive Comments" and "Negative Comments" are collected. In all the 30 shops, "Positive Comments" generally account for around 80% of total comments. "Negative Comments" are also chosen in order to see the differences between describing good taste and bad taste, if there are any.

After the restaurants and comments are decided, a third-party web crawler *Octoparse* (*Bazhuayu* in Chinese) is used to scrape the data from the website automatically. With repeated comments excluded, 85,318 positive comments versus 4,007 negative comments were collected as at 8 June 2018. Two corpora, Positive Comments Corpus (hereinafter referred to as 'PCC') and Negative Comments Corpus (hereinafter referred to as 'NCC'), are compiled in the *Sketch Engine* (Kilgarriff *et al.*, 2004), with words segmented and parts-of-speech tagged. This has generated 4,524,812 tokens in PCC and 260,551 tokens for NCC. Functions in the *Sketch Engine* (Kilgarriff *et al.*, 2004) are used to further examine the data so as to address the above three research questions.

4 Results and Discussion

4.1 Description of Desserts

Firstly, a word list is generated to examine the overall frequency of the vocabulary appearing in PCC. Appendix A presents top 10 frequent words related to tasting experience across three main lexical categories. As indicated by the word frequency, verbs appear much less frequently as compared to nouns and adjectives when describing tasting experience. In terms of adjectives, 甜 (*tián*, 'sweet'), 腻 (*nì*, 'fatty/get tired of'), 新鲜 (*xīnxiān*, 'fresh'), 濃郁 (*nóngyù*, 'rich/strong'), and 香 (*xiāng*, 'fragrant/delicious') are the most concrete ones which are related to the feelings of tasting, but it is not known whether these were used to describe desserts only. With regard to nouns, apart from the specific foods or drinks mentioned in the comments, we have spotted three most frequently used terms which directly relate to the research questions in this paper, i.e., 味道 *wèidao*, 口味 *kǒuwèi* and 口感 *kǒugǎn*.

As discussed in the Introduction, 味道 *wèidao* could be understood as taste, smell as well as flavour in English. However, 口味 (*kǒuwèi*, 'one's taste/flavour') and 口感 (*kǒugǎn*, 'mouthfeel') are

sites worldwide to provide restaurant, shopping, entertainment, leisure and day to day living services through its interactive platform. Accessed at http://www.dianping.com/.

[7] Meituan was a Chinese group buying website and was merged with Dazhong Dianping in 2015 and is now known as Meituan-Dianping.

also related to taste and flavour of food to some degree. In fact, when using the "Thesaurus" function to generate a list of words similar to 味道 *wèidao*, 口味 *kǒuwèi* ranks the highest with a similarity score of 0.471 and 口感 *kǒugǎn* ranks third with a score of 0.43. In order to differentiate between the three frequently used nouns as well as the near-synonymous pairs, "Word Sketch Difference" is applied to explore the common and exclusive patterns for the three words. With the "Word Sketch" function, the *Sketch Engine* automatically extracts collocations based on grammatical patterns and the collocations are ranked by MI log Frequency (previously known as "salience") (Kilgarriff *et al.*, 2004).

From the patterns of the three words shown in Appendix B, C and D (only the keyword under 'subject' and 'modifiers' are shown due to limited space),味道 *wèidao* is found to be more collocated with gustatory and olfactory vocabulary. Two typical words shown in Appendix B to describe 味道 *wèidao* are 濃 (*nóng*, 'of intense taste') and 淡 (*dàn*, 'of mild taste'). As for 口味 *kǒuwèi,* we can 選擇 (*xuǎnzé*, 'to choose') or 嘗試 (*chángshì*, 'to try') particular 口味 (*kǒuwèi*, 'flavour') and we have our 個人口味 (*gèrén kǒuwèi*, 'personal taste'). With regard to 口感 (*kǒugǎn*, 'mouthfeel'), a bunch of tactile terms are listed in Appendix D, and several frequently used terms are 脆 (*cuì*, 'crisp'), 乾 (*gān*, 'dry'), 滑 (*huá*, 'smooth'), 酥 (*sū*, 'crunchy') and 軟 (*ruǎn*, 'soft/tender'). The differences among these three near-synonyms suggest that descriptions for desserts tend to be more frequently collocated with 口感 (*kǒugǎn*, 'mouthfeel'). 'Mouthfeel' is claimed to be a term for the sensory perception which is closely related to taste and aroma but is greatly influenced by "the structure, texture and responsible for the overall impression of the food" (Mouritsen & Styrbæk, 2014, p.6). It is considered a new word which only became prevalent in recent years (only three instances of 'mouthfeel' can be found in BNC corpus[8] while 1,679 tokens exist in English Web 2015 corpus). Nevertheless, that the descriptors of desserts are most likely related to 口感 (*kǒugǎn*, 'mouthfeel') rather than 味道 (*wèidao*, 'taste/smell/flavour') is consistent with Jurafsky (2014)'s discussion of vocabulary describing desserts in English, in which it is not our gustatory or olfactory but the tactile sense that plays a major role.

To examine the most frequent vocabulary related to 'mouthfeel' of desserts in the corpus and to address the first research question, 口感 (*kǒugǎn*, 'mouthfeel') is set as the KWIC (key word in context) and is searched in both the PCC and NCC. Due to a large number of 口感 (*kǒugǎn*, 'mouthfeel') existed in the PCC (5,928 instances), only 口感 (*kǒugǎn*, 'mouthfeel') that acts as the subject and the object being modified in the sentence are further examined manually.

In 1,734 concordances containing the keyword 口感 (*kǒugǎn*, 'mouthfeel') in the PCC, 175 words (types) and 1325 tokens were identified, including 138 monosyllabic and disyllabic adjectives (Top 20 are shown in **Table 1** below), 5 ABB adjectives (e.g. 軟綿綿 *ruǎnmiánmián*, 'soft', 硬邦邦 *yìngbāngbāng*, 'hard', 甜津津 *tiánjīnjīn*, 'sweet'), 6 four-word conventionalized phrases (e.g. 入口即化 *rù-kǒu-jí-huà*, 'melts in one's mouth', 甜而不膩 *tián-ér-bù-nì*, 'acceptably sweet', 外脆內軟 *wài-cuì-nèi-ruǎn,* 'crunchy/crispy outside and tender inside'), 4 nouns (層次 *céngcì*, 'layer', 嚼勁 *jiáojìn*, 'chewiness', 韌性 *rènxìng*, 'rubbery', 彈性 *tánxìng*, 'bouncy'), 5 verbs (回甘 *huígān*, 'turns from bitterness to sweetness', 帶甘 *dàigān*, 'with sweetness', 爆漿 *bàojiāng*, 'molten', 層疊 *céngdié*, 'layer', 刺激 *cìji*, 'stimulating'), 4 onomatopoeia (咯吱咯吱 *gēzhī-gēzhī*, 'crunching sound', 沙沙 *shāshā*, 'rustling sound', 咂咂 *zāzā*, 'smacking sound', duaiduai 'bounce sound'), 9 dialect words (e.g. Q 'chewy', Q 彈 *Q-tán* 'chewy', 紮實 *zhāshi*, 'solid', 面 *miàn*, 'mushy', 粉 *fěn*, 'mushy'), and 4 English words (heavy, creamy, juicy, fresh).

Word	Tokens	Word	Tokens
1 甜 *tián* 'sweet'	89	2 膩 *nì* 'get tired of'	67
3 濃郁 *nóngyù* 'rich/strong'	59	4 脆 *cuì* 'crisp'	57
5 清爽 *qīngshuǎng* 'refreshing'	43	6 豐富 *fēngfù* 'rich'	43
7 苦 *kǔ* 'bitter'	42	8 鬆軟 *sōngruǎn* 'fluffy'	41
9 酥脆 *sūcuì*	39	10 酸 *suān*	28

[8] BNC corpus was created in the 1980s – early 1990s.

'crisp/crunchy'		'sour'	
11 細膩 *xìnì* 'fine and smooth'	28	12 硬 *yìng* 'hard'	27
13 綿密 *miánmì* 'creamy'	27	14 甜膩 *tiánnì* 'sweet'	26
15 淡 *dàn* 'of mild taste'	26	16 清新 *qīngxīn* 'fresh'	25
17 乾 *gān* 'dry'	24	18 香 *xiāng* 'fragrant/ delicious'	21
19 新鮮 *xīnxiān* 'fresh'	20	20 軟 *ruǎn* 'soft/tender'	18

Table 1 - Top 20 monosyllabic and disyllabic adjectives describing 'mouthfeel' of desserts in PCC

On the other hand, NCC only contains 175 concordances with the keyword 口感 (*kǒugǎn*, 'mouthfeel'). 31 words (types) and 46 tokens were found as the 'mouthfeel' of desserts (Top 10 are shown in **Table 2** below as the frequency is quite low after the first ten words), in which, 4 of them are ABB adjectives (two not in the PCC are 乾巴巴 *gānbābā* 'dry' and 黏糊糊 *niánhuhu* 'sticky'), 2 four-word conventionalized phrases (淡而無味 *dàn-ér-wú-wèi* 'tasteless' and 甜而不膩 *tián-ér-bù-nì* 'acceptably sweet'), 1 dialect word (擰唧唧 'mushy'), and the remaining 24 words are all monosyllabic and disyllabic adjectives. PCC and NCC share most of the common 'mouthfeel' vocabulary, with only 7 terms in NCC could not be found in PCC, including 糊 (*hú*, 'mushy'), 空 (*kōng*, 'empty'), 遲鈍 (*chídùn*, 'dull'), 高冷 (*gāolěng*, 'arrogant') and the above-mentioned 2 ABB adjectives and a four-word conventionalized phrase (i.e.淡而無味 *dàn-ér-wú-wèi*, 'tasteless').

Word	Tokens	Word	Tokens
1 硬 *yìng* 'hard'	5	2 粗糙 *cūcāo* 'coarse'	4
3 乾巴巴 *gānbābā* 'dry'	3	4 甜 *tián* 'sweet'	2
5 軟綿綿 *ruǎnmiánmián* 'soft'	2	6 膩 *nì* 'get tired of'	2
7 淡 *dàn* 'of mild taste'	2	8 醇厚 *chúnhòu* 'mellow'	2
9 新鮮 *xīnxiān* 'fresh'	2	10 酥軟 *sūruǎn*, 'crunchy and soft'	1

Table 2 - Top 10 monosyllabic and disyllabic adjectives describing 'mouthfeel' of desserts in NCC

Comparing the vocabulary used to describe good and bad taste/flavour of desserts in Chinese, it is found that very few items are directly associated with negative valence - 硬 (*yìng*, 'hard'), 粗糙 (*cūcāo*, 'coarse'), 乾 (*gān*, 'dry') and 膩 (*nì*, 'get tired of') are possibly the only four items mainly generate negative feelings. In these, 膩 (*nì*, 'get tired of') is an interesting word which is hard to locate its equivalent in English. Most of the 膩 (*nì*, 'get tired of') in the DESSERT corpus do not mean 'fatty' or 'greasy', but it is more like the sick feeling when you feel something is too sweet or get tired of eating too much sweet or greasy stuff. For example:

a. 濃郁的巧克力包裹著鬆軟的蛋糕，軟硬適中，口感絲滑醇厚卻不**甜膩**。
Nóngyù de qiǎokèlì bāoguǒ zhe sōngruǎn
Rich DE chocolate wrap ZHE fluffy
de dàngāo, ruǎnyìng shìzhòng, kǒugǎn
DE cake soft-hard moderate mouthfeel
sīhuá chúnhòu què bù tiánnì.
smooth mellow however not sweet-ni
'Rich chocolate wrapped with fluffy cakes, moderate hardness, soft and mellow but not too sweet.'

b. 抹茶芝士蛋糕的奶酪味好厚重，吃起來好滿足，但一塊下來就會有點**膩**。
Mǒchá zhīshì dàngāo de nǎilào wèi hǎo
Matcha cheese cake DE cheese taste very
hòuzhòng, chī qǐlái hǎo mǎnzú, dàn yī
thick eat up very satisfied but one
kuài xiàlái jiù huì yǒudiǎn nì.
piece down then will a bit ni
'The cheese of Matcha cheesecake is very thick and very yummy, but we got a bit tired of it after finishing the piece.'

The DESSERT corpus demonstrates that most of the time people will just add negative structures to the positive words to express their dislikes, such as 不… (*bù…*, 'not…') and 太…了 (*tài…le*, 'too…'), as follows:

c. 鬆餅賣相不錯，可惜**不**脆，軟軟的。
Sōngbǐng màixiàng bùcuò, kěxī bù cuì,
Muffin sell-look not-bad pity not crispy
ruǎn ruǎn de.
soft soft DE
'The muffin looks good, but unfortunately it is not crispy, too soft.'

d. 布朗尼口感還不錯，但**太**甜了。
Bùlăngní kǒugăn hái bùcuò,
Brownie mouthfeel relative not bad
dàn tài tián le.
but too sweet-LE
'Brownie tastes good, but too sweet.'

To sum up, concerning the descriptions of taste and flavour of desserts, it is found that vocabulary describing 口感 (*kǒugăn*, 'mouthfeel') is much more relevant than those for 味道 (*wèidao*, 'taste/smell/flavour') or 口味 (*kǒuwèi*, 'one's taste/flavour), as evidenced by the hundreds of 'mouthfeel' words identified. Most of these terms are adjectives and people tend to combine 'preferred' morphemes to make up compound words to describe their 'preferable' taste and flavour, such as three morphemes 甜 (*tián*, 'sweet'), 香 (*xiāng*, 'fragrant/delicious') and 滑 (*huá*, 'smooth') in the compound words 香甜 (*xiāngtián*, 'delicious and sweet'), 甜滑 (*tiánhuá*, 'sweet and smooth') and 香滑 (*xiānghuá*, 'delicious and smooth'). In addition, compared to the overwhelmingly positive words of describing desserts, negative words are rare in Chinese, and this is consistent with Jurafsky (2014)'s discussion mentioned previously.

4.2 Interrelation among sensory modalities

As mentioned in the discussion in the Introduction, 'flavour' denotes the integrated effect of taste and smell sensations, as well as mouthfeel and chemesthesis[9] in the oral cavity (Mouritsen & Styrbæk, 2017, p.5). In the foregoing part, 'mouthfeel' is seen as critical when discussing desserts. Klosse (2014, p.38) claimed that "there is no flavour without some kind of mouthfeel" and 'mouthfeel' is considered the "major determinants of consumer acceptance and preference for foods and beverages" (Guinard & Mazzucchelli, 1996, p.213). Given the importance of 'mouthfeel' in desserts, in this section, some linguistic evidence in the DESSERT corpus will be presented for the purpose of discussing the interactions among sensory modalities.

In all of the 182 'mouthfeel' words identified in the previous section, around 80 of them belong to tactile sensation (~44%), rendering them as 'synaesthetic metaphors' to depict TASTE of desserts. The identification of synaesthetic metaphors mainly follows Zhao, Xiong and Huang (2018)'s methodology of studying linguistic synaesthesia in Chinese, i.e., to classify the sensory vocabulary into five senses (vision, hearing, smell, taste and touch), to check the etymology of the word, and to determine if the word has extended meaning of describing other sensory modalities. In regard to these synaesthetic metaphors, first of all, they belong to the tactile sense as they can be sensed by tactile receptors, including mechanoreceptors (which pick up sensations like pressure, vibration and texture), thermoreceptors (related to temperature like hot and cold), pain receptors, and proprioceptors (deep pressure sense felt by muscles, tendons and joints when we make movements) (Popova, 2005); secondly, they are all used to describe feelings in the mouth, i.e., tastes and flavours. In particular, it is found that taste/flavour of desserts is largely influenced by the texture - 脆 (*cuì*, 'crisp'), 滑 (*huá*, 'smooth'), 粗 (*cū*, 'coarse'), 黏 (*nián*, 'sticky'), 軟 (*ruăn*, 'soft'), to name a few. Temperature also plays a part but instead of the two polarities, hot and cold, the temperature-related items are all rather 'pleasant' feelings, like 溫 (*wēn*, 'warm'), 暖 (*nuăn*, 'warm'), 冰 (*bīng*, 'icy'), and 涼 (*liáng*, 'cool'). This may indicate that desserts should preferably be at a mild and moderate temperature rather than being hot or cold.

Apart from the tactile vocabulary, around 20 'mouthfeel' items were defined as gustatory terms, which are in line with basic five taste qualities defined neurologically, including *sour*, *sweet*, *salty*, *bitter* and *umami*[10] (Mouritsen & Styrbæk, 2014), and words originally denoting taste sense, like 濃 (*nóng*, 'of intense taste'), 淡 (*dàn*, 'of mild taste'), 醇 (*chún*, 'pure'), and 美味 (*měiwèi*, 'tasty')[11]. Interestingly, olfactory (smell) terms are not found in the descriptions of 'mouthfeel' of desserts,

[9] Chemesthesis belongs to tactile sense that relies on the same receptor mechanisms as those that convey pain, touch and temperature on the skin.

[10] It is a word in Japanese which combines the ideas of *umai* "delicious" and *mi* "essence" and known as 鮮 *xiān* in Mandarin Chinese.

[11] Original meanings of these words were checked in *ShuoWenJieZi* in *Handian*. Accessed at http://www.zdic.net/.

except one olfactory word 香 (*xiāng*, 'fragrant/delicious'). But this word has limited smell connotation in DESSERT corpus. Instead, it transfers to the taste sense, meaning tasty or delicious. Indeed, taste and smell are closely intertwined in a way that perception of taste is apparently induced by odours and gustatory terms are also used to describe odours (Auvray & Spence, 2008).

In addition, it is found that VISION and HEARING have the tendency to transfer to TASTE of desserts as well[12]. Visual items including 薄 (*báo*, 'mild'), 清澈 (*qīngchè*, 'clear'), 層次 (*céngcì*, layer), 蓬鬆 (*péngsōng*, 'fluffy'), 濃密 (*nóngmì*, 'thick/dense'), 乾淨 (*gānjìng*, 'clean') and etc., and auditory terms involving onomatopoetic words as shown previously both suggest that flavour perception is multisensory, it integrates all the five sensory modalities, although to varying degrees.

4.3 Conceptualization of desserts

The last but not least research question being addressed is how DESSERT is represented and conceptualized in Chinese culture. It is known that the main purpose of desserts is to make people happy rather than to nourish the body. Neurological studies suggest that sweet foods are highly desirable due to the powerful impact sugar has on the reward system in the brain, which is the same area that drugs and sexual behaviour activate (Avena, 2014). This is perhaps the reason why, in English and many other languages, words expressing sensuality and sexuality are dominant when used to describe good desserts. However, in Chinese, where explicit sensual expressions are not encouraged, some metaphorical expressions are found noteworthy for discussion, such as:

a. …醇厚的口感中帶些清新**調皮**…
…*chúnhòu de kǒugǎn zhōng dài xiē qīngxīn tiáopí…*
mello DE mouthfeel in with some freshness naughty
'...mellow taste with some freshness and naughtiness...'

b. …口感不雜，不**浮誇**。
…*kǒugǎn bù zá, bù fúkuā.*
mouthfeel not mixed not boastful
'…the taste is not mixed, and not boastful.'

c. …口感很充實**硬朗**…
…*kǒugǎn hěn chōngshí yìnglǎng…*
mouthfeel very rich tough
'...the taste is very rich and tough...'

Words highlighted in bold imply that desserts can be conceptualized as a person's personality in Chinese, and often a pleasant one. On the contrary, 遲鈍 (*chídùn*, 'dull') and 高冷 (*gāolěng*, 'arrogant'), deemed as unpleasant personalities, are used to describe bad taste. These adjectives stem from impressions of personalities gained through social interactional contact. Thus, personifying delicious desserts as pleasant characters using such positive adjectives illustrates that, in Chinese culture, language emanating from social interactional experience, rather than feeling of physical bodily pleasure only, is also used to describe desserts.

5 Conclusion

Despite the fact that tasting is a subjective experience, with the online corpus consisting of reviews of food and restaurants, we can explore how people perceive foods in reality. Focusing on the descriptions of DESSERT in Chinese, this study has revealed that 'mouthfeel' is more often discussed than 'taste' or 'smell' when desserts are mentioned in Chinese. As 'mouthfeel' mostly consists of tactile vocabulary and is influenced by gustatory, visual and auditory terms to some extent, this paper further provides manifestations for linguistic synaesthesia in which TASTE can be treated as a target domain and other sensory domains all have impacts on it.

This study could be replicated to investigate descriptions of other types of food in Chinese, with an emphasis on looking into how sensory modalities are interrelated. Comparisons between Chinese and other languages on food also need to be undertaken in order to unveil cultural differences in this subject.

[12] Note this tendency does not show in Zhao, Xiong and Huang (2018)'s directionality of linguistic synaesthesia in Chinese. It is likely that the instantiations of VISION and HEARING transferring to TASTE are not frequent and common in Mandarin Chinese.

References

Ankerstein, Carrie A. & Pereira, Gerardine M. (2013). Talking about taste: starved for words. In Gerhardt, C., Frobenius, M., & Ley, S. (Eds.), *Culinary Linguistics: The Chef's Special* (pp.305-315). Amsterdam: John Benjamins Publishing Company.

Auvray, Malika & Spence, Charles. (2008). The multisensory perception of flavor. *Consciousness and Cognition, 17*(3), 1016-1031.

Avena, Nicole. (2014, January). Nicole Avena: How sugar affects the brain [Video file]. Retrieved from https://www.ted.com/talks/nicole_avena_how_sugar_affects_the_brain

Backhouse, Anthony Edgar. (1994). *The lexical field of taste: a semantic study of Japanese taste terms*. Cambridge: Cambridge University Press.

Guinard, Jean-Xavier & Mazzucchelli, Rossella. (1996). The sensory perception of texture and mouthfeel. *Trends in Food Science & Technology, 7*(7), 213-219.

Han, Shaogong. (1996). Zhong Xi ge you qi "tian" [Different "sweet" in Chinese and Western]. *Frontiers* (2), 11-12.

Jurafsky, Dan. (2014). *The language of food: a linguist reads the menu*. New York: W.W. Norton & Company.

Kilgarriff, Adam, Vít Baisa, Jan Bušta, Miloš Jakubíček, Vojtěch Kovář, Jan Michelfeit, Pavel Rychlý & Vít Suchomel. (2014). The sketch engine: Ten years on. *Lexicography, 1*(1), 7–36.

Klosse, Peter. (2014). *The essence of gastronomy: understanding the flavor of foods and beverages*. Boca Raton, Florida: CRC Press, Taylor & Francis Group.

Knoblock, John & Riegel, Jeffrey. (2000). *The annals of Lü Buwei*. Stanford, California: Stanford University Press.

Mouritsen, Ole G. & Styrbæk, Klavs. (2014). *Umami: unlocking the secrets of the fifth taste*. New York: Columbia University Press.

Mouritsen, Ole G. & Styrbæk, Klavs. (2017). *Mouthfeel: how texture makes taste*. New York: Columbia University Press.

Popova, Yanna. (2005). Image schemas and verbal synaesthesia. In Hampe, Beate (Ed.), *From Perception to Meaning: Image Schemas in Cognitive Linguistics* (pp. 395-420). Berlin: de Gruyter.

Small, Dana M. (2012). Flavor is in the brain. *Physiology and Behavior, 107*(4), 540-552.

Spence, Charles. (2017). Multisensory flavour perception. In Guichard, E., & Salles, C., Morzel, M., & Le Bon, A. (Eds.), *Flavour: From Food to Perception* (pp.373-394). West Sussex, UK & Hoboken, USA: John Wiley & Sons, Ltd.

Strauss, Susan. (2005). The linguistic aestheticization of food: a cross-cultural look at food commercials in Japan, Korea, and the United States. *Journal of Pragmatics, 37*(9), 1427-1455.

Strik Lievers, Francesca & Winter, Bodo. (2018). Sensory language across lexical categories. *Lingua*, 204, 45-61.

Ullmann, Stephen. (1957). *The principles of semantics*. Oxford: Basil Blackwell.

Williams, Joseph. (1976). Synaesthetic adjectives: a possible law of sematic change. *Language, 52* (2), 461-478.

Winter, Bodo. (2016a). *The sensory structure of the English lexicon*. (PhD Thesis), University of California, Merced, United States.

Winter, Bodo. (2016b). Taste and smell words form an affectively loaded and emotionally flexible part of the English lexicon. *Language, Cognition and Neuroscience, 31*(8), 975-988.

Wu, Tieping. (1989). Butong yuyan de weijueci he wenduci dui keguan xianshi de butong qiefen - yuyan leixingxue yanjiu [Different categorizations in the world through gustatory and temperature words in different languages - a typological study]. *Language Teaching and Linguistic Studies*(01), 120-137.

Xiong, Jiajuan & Huang, Chu-Ren. (2016). The synaesthetic and metaphorical uses of 味 wei'taste' in Chinese Buddhist texts. In Proceedings of 30th *Pacific Asia Conference on Language, Information and Computation (PACLIC 30)*, 485-492.

Zhao, Qingqing, Huang, Chu-Ren & Long, Yunfei. (2018). Synaesthesia in Chinese: A corpus-based study on gustatory adjectives in Mandarin. To appear in *Linguistics*.

Zhao, Qingqing, Xiong, Jiajuan & Huang, Chu-Ren. (2018). Tonggan, yinyu yu renzhi: tonggan xianxiang zai Hanyu zhong de xitongxing biaoxian yu yuyanxue jiazhi [Synaesthesia, metaphor and cognition: systematic representations of synaesthesia in Chinese and its linguistic values]. To appear in *Studies of the Chinese Language*.

Appendices

Nouns		Adjectives		Verbs	
Word	**Frequency**	**Word**	**Frequency**	**Word**	**Frequency**
咖啡 *kāfēi*, 'coffee'	30,379	好 *hǎo*, 'good'	38,866	吃 *chī*, 'to eat'	27,752
蛋糕 *dàngāo*, 'cake'	17,672	不錯 *bùcuò*, 'not bad'	36,280	感覺 *gǎnjué*, 'to feel'	15,336
味道 *wèidao*, 'taste/smell/flavour'	25,240	好吃 *hǎochī*, 'tasty'	18,749	喝 *hē*, 'to drink'	14,775
巧克力 *qiǎokèlì*, 'chocolate'	11,593	一般 *yībān*, 'alright'	9,128	烘焙 *hōngbèi*, 'to bake'	2,621
口味 *kǒuwèi*, 'one's taste/flavour'	8,142	甜 *tián*, 'sweet'	8,301	嘗試 *chángshì*, 'to try'	2,183
甜品 *tiánpǐn*, 'dessert'	6,126	好喝 *hǎohē*, 'good to drink'	5,113	體驗 *tǐyàn*, 'to experience'	2,175
抹茶 *mǒchá*, 'matcha'	6,072	膩 *nì*, 'fatty/get tired of'	4,245	配 *pèi*, 'to go with'	2,030
口感 *kǒugǎn*, 'mouthfeel'	5,928	新鮮 *xīnxiān*, 'fresh'	2,715	搭配 *dāpèi*, 'to go with'	1,877
麵包 *miànbāo*, 'bread'	5,721	濃郁 *nóngyù*, 'rich/strong'	2,677	煙熏 *yānxūn*, 'smoked'	1,752
拿鐵 *Nátiě*, 'Latte'	5,392	香 *xiāng*, 'fragrant/delicious'	2,338	品嘗 *pǐncháng*, 'to try'	1,167

Appendix A. Top 10 frequent words related to tasting experience across three main lexical categories

Subject	Frequency	MI log Frequency	Modifiers (including Adjective Modifiers and Noun Modifiers)	Frequency	MI log Frequency
很好 *hěnhǎo*, 'very good'	57	8.2	抹茶 *mǒchá*, 'matcha'	60	10.1
好 *hǎo*, 'good'	40	7.7	濃郁 *nóngyù*, 'rich/strong'	42	9.4
不過不失 *bù-guò-bù-shī*, 'alright'	31	7.4	淡淡 *dàndàn*, 'of mild taste'	32	9.0
膩/不膩 *nì/bù nì*, 'fatty/not fatty'; 'tired of/not tired of'	21	6.8	特別 *tèbié*, 'special'	27	8.8
不錯 *bùcuò*, 'not bad'	18	6.7	濃濃 *nóngnóng*, 'of intense taste'	27	8.7

Appendix B. 味道 (*wèidao*, 'taste/smell/flavour') only patterns (first 5 words)

Subject	Frequency	MI log Frequency	Modifiers (including Adjective Modifiers and Noun Modifiers)	Frequency	MI log Frequency
選擇 *xuǎnzé*, 'choice'	42	9.1	個人 *gèrén*, 'personal'	131	10.9
選 *xuǎn*, 'to choose'	20	8.1	我的 *wǒ de*, 'my'	94	10.6
可選 *kě xuǎn*, 'can choose'	12	7.7	新 *xīn*, 'new'	6	8.5
嘗試 *chángshì*, 'to try'	14	7.7	沒有 *méiyǒu*, 'no'	5	8.5
保持 *bǎochí*, 'to keep'	10	7.4	甜膩 *tiánnì*, 'sweet'	5	8.4

Appendix C. 口味 (*kǒuwèi*, 'one's taste/flavour') only patterns (first 5 words)

Subject	Frequency	MI log Frequency	Modifiers (including Adjective Modifiers and Noun Modifiers)	Frequency	MI log Frequency
乾 *gān*, 'dry'	12	8.3	脆 *cuì*, 'crisp'	14	9.3
順滑 *shùnhuá*, 'smooth'	7	7.7	酥脆 *sūcuì*, 'crunchy'	14	9.3
細滑 *xìhuá*, 'fine and smooth'	6	7.5	鬆軟 *sōngruǎn*, 'fluffy'	12	9.1
綿綿 *miánmián*, 'spongy'	5	7.2	脆脆 *cuìcuì*, 'crisp'	12	9.1
酥軟 *sūruǎn*, 'crunchy and soft'	5	7.2	膩 *nì*, 'fatty/get tired of'	9	8.6

Appendix D. 口感 (*kǒugǎn*, 'mouthfeel') only patterns (first 5 words)

AUTHOR INDEX

Association for Computational Linguistics
209 N. Eighth Street
Stroudsburg, Pennsylvania 18360

ISBN 978-1-5108-8907-1

9 781510 889071

CURRAN ASSOCIATES INC.
proceedings.com